A Resource Book for Improving Principals' Learning-Centered Leadership

---

This book is part of the Peter Lang Education list.
Every volume is peer reviewed and meets
the highest quality standards for content and production.

PETER LANG
New York • Washington, D.C./Baltimore • Bern
Frankfurt • Berlin • Brussels • Vienna • Oxford

A Resource Book for Improving Principals' Learning-Centered Leadership

EDITED BY JIANPING SHEN
& VAN E. COOLEY

PETER LANG
New York • Washington, D.C./Baltimore • Bern
Frankfurt • Berlin • Brussels • Vienna • Oxford

Library of Congress Cataloging-in-Publication Data

A resource book for improving principals' learning-centered leadership /
edited by Jianping Shen, Van E. Cooley.
pages cm
Includes bibliographical references and index.
1. School principals. 2. Learning. 3. Educational leadership.
I. Shen, Jianping, editor of compilation. II. Cooley, Van, editor of compilation.
LB2831.9.R47 371.2'012—dc23 2012050308
ISBN 978-1-4331-1576-9 (hardcover)
ISBN 978-1-4331-1575-2 (paperback)
ISBN 978-1-4539-0930-0 (e-book)

Bibliographic information published by **Die Deutsche Nationalbibliothek**.
Die Deutsche Nationalbibliothek lists this publication in the "Deutsche Nationalbibliografie"; detailed bibliographic data is available on the Internet at http://dnb.d-nb.de/.

The paper in this book meets the guidelines for permanence and durability of the Committee on Production Guidelines for Book Longevity of the Council of Library Resources.

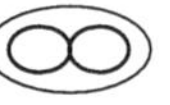

29 Broadway, 18th floor, New York, NY 10006
www.peterlang.com

Printed in the United States of America

Dedication

In Memory of Dr. Van E. Cooley

Van Edwin Cooley, Ed.D., was a lifelong learner, advocate for education reform, respected educator, beloved family member and treasured friend. He worked in the field of education for 38 years, serving as a teacher, vice principal, assistant superintendent and superintendent in Indiana, and as an associate professor, professor, department chair and interim dean at Western Michigan University. Dr. Cooley authored or co-authored over 60 scholarly articles and directed or co-directed numerous grants. His memory will live on in the lives that he touched.

Table of Contents

1 Introduction

JIANPING SHEN AND VAN E. COOLEY

Principalship makes a difference for the school, the teachers, and the students. Principalship has been evolving, and principals currently face a multitude of challenges with improved student achievement at the top of the list. This volume is a resource book for principals, focusing on seven important dimensions of their work: (1) data-informed decision-making, (2) safe and orderly school operation, (3) high, cohesive, and culturally relevant expectations for students, (4) distributive and empowering leadership, (5) coherent curricular programs, (6) real-time and embedded instructional assessment, and (7) passion for and commitment to school renewal. It seeks to provide a research base, best practice, and tools for principals along these seven dimensions.

In this chapter, we briefly trace the evolution of school principalship and describe current challenges facing principals. We then document that principals do make a difference and tease out the seven important dimensions of their work. Finally we describe the organization of the book so that readers can find the information they need efficiently.

The Evolution of Principalship

Principalship has evolved over the years. Weiss (1992) observed that the position was created in response to emerging factors such as the growth of urban populations, the change from one-room ungraded schools to graded ones, and removal of the principal's teaching duties. Beck and Murphy (1993) studied the history of principalship and developed Table 1.1 to illustrate the major themes of its evolution from the 1920s to 1980s.

Table 1.1 Evolution of Principalship

Decade	Metaphorical Phrase	Description
1920s	Value Broker	Leader of a parish
1930s	Scientific Manager	Business executive focusing on budgeting, maintenance, and accounting
1940s	Democratic Leader	A coordinator who works cooperatively with teachers
1950s	Theory-Guided Administrator	Synthesizer who accomplishes the goals of both scientific management (organizational purpose) and human relations (individual purpose)
1960s	Bureaucratic Executive	Using scientific method to reach measurable outcomes
1970s	Humanistic Facilitator	Team player who respects teachers and influences others by involving them in the school
1980s	Instructional Leader	Directly involved in the teaching and learning process to improve student achievement
1990s	Boundary Spanner	Reaching out to the community in order to maintain enrollment and improve achievement due to the increasing diversity and competition from charter schools and vouchers
2000s	Champion for school improvement	Becoming accountable for school improvement

The entries up to the 1980s were adapted from Beck and Murphy (1993). The metaphorical themes were those dominant in each decade. However, as will be discussed later, these themes do not disappear. Rather, they are "layered" one on another over time.

The development of the educational scene seems to suggest that principalship will continue to evolve. It is fair to say that student achievement and accountability remain as the themes of principalship for this century. When Portin and Shen (1998, 2005) studied the position in the state of Washington in the mid-1990s, they found four phenomena related to principalship. The first is "layering": New responsibilities have been added to the role. However, traditional responsibilities—such as keeping a safe school, interacting with parents and community, managing the budget—have not been shifted. Furthermore, new responsibilities do not always come with new resources to support the new roles. Table 1.1 also illustrated the phenomenon of layering. From decade to decade, additional responsibilities have been added to principals' jobs.

The second phenomenon is "shifting from leadership to management." Principals have been asked to take leadership roles in developing a vision for improving their school but also in maintaining managerial roles of budgeting and disciplining. Managerial roles tend to be more visible, and lack of attention to them brings immediate repercussions. Therefore, many principals tend to prioritize managerial over leadership roles. Some principals feel they do not have enough time to do both.

The third phenomenon is "ambiguity and complexity." New responsibilities for principals tend to be ambiguous. Portin and Shen (1998, 2005) found the decentralization initiative does not clearly spell out authority at the district and school levels. Furthermore, principals feel that they do not have the skills or support to "market" their schools—another new responsibility—to an increasingly diverse and critical population. The layering of traditional and new, ambiguous responsibilities, coupled with an increasingly critical stakeholder group, augments the complexity of the job.

As a result of the first three points, the fourth phenomenon is "declining morale and enthusiasm." Many principals feel increased frustration and decreased security and enthusiasm. Principals actually welcome the changes. However, declining morale and enthusiasm is caused by the absence of support, the inability to play both managerial and leadership roles effectively and efficiently, and the lack of appreciation for their work.

The four phenomena related to principalship will most likely continue as the position evolves and additional responsibilities continue to be added. With the continuing development of responsibilities, there is a need to have a parsimonious model for researchers to establish a typology to study principalship and to allow the practitioners to talk about their work in a cogent and meaningful way. Comparing the Interstate School Leaders Licensure Consortium (ISLLC) Standards for School Leaders of 1996 and 2008, we perceive a tendency toward a more parsimonious model of responsibilities for school leaders, including principals (please see the comparison between 1996 and 2008 ISLLC standards in the 2008 Standards, Council of Chief State School Officers, 2008). In the 1996 ISLLC version, there were 6 standards and 183 items for "knowledge, skills, and dispositions," while in the 2008 ISLLC version, there were still 6 standards but only 31 "functions." Given the current emphasis on student achievement and accountability, we developed a typology of seven dimensions of principalship with a focus on student learning.

Principals' Impact on School Improvement[1]

According to Leithwood, Louis, Anderson, and Wahlstrom (2004), leadership is second only to classroom instruction among school-related factors that affect student learning, accounting for about 25% of total direct and indirect effects on student learning. The common core of basic leadership practices includes "setting directions," "developing people," and "redesigning the organization to develop one that supports the performance of administrators, teachers, and students." Through empirical research, we know much about the principalship (Cooley & Shen, 2000, 2003; Rodriguez-Campo, Rincones-Gomez, & Shen, 2005; Shen & Crawford, 2003; Shen, Cooley, & Wegenke, 2004; Shen, Kavanaugh, Wegenke, Rodriguez-Campos, Rincones-Gomez, Palmer, Crawford, Cooley, Poppink, VanderJagt, Hsieh, Ruhl-Smith, Keiser, & Portin, 2005), particularly the dimensions that affect student learning. For example, researchers found that the impact of the principalship centers on the role of shaping the school's instructional climate and instructional organization (Bossert, Dwyer, Rowan, & Lee, 1982; Goldring & Pasternak, 1994; Hallinger, Bickman, & Davis, 1996; Heck, Larson, & Marcoulides, 1990; Leithwood & Jantzi, 1999). Instructional climate includes, among other areas, the culture for school renewal (Sebring & Bryk, 2000; Smith, Guarino, Strom, & Adams, 2006), distributive and empowering leadership (Marks & Printy, 2003), high expectations for students (Cotton, 2003), and data-informed decision-making (Celio & Harvey, 2005; Shen, Cooley, Reeves, Burt, Ryan, Rainey, & Yuan, 2010; Shen, Cooley, Ma, Reeves, Burt, Rainey, & Yuan, 2012). Research by Marcoulides and Heck (1993) and O'Donnell and White (2005) indicated that the principal's leadership in building the instructional climate and organizing the instructional program is a significant predictor for academic achievement. Other studies by Heck and Marcoulides (1992) and Hallinger (1992) suggested that the principals' leadership appears to be exercised primarily through behaviors that shape the school-level instructional framework such as managing the instructional program and promoting a positive learning climate.

Subsequent studies conducted by Lee and Smith (1996), Louis, Marks, and Kruse (1996), Marks and Louis (1997), and Manthey (2006) also documented significant positive effects on achievement associated with principal leadership that shapes a strong professional community and collective responsibility for student learning. Principals' instructional leadership encompasses many factors such as promoting effective pedagogies, including, among others, (a) culturally relevant pedagogy (Boykin & Cunningham, 2001; Ladson-Billings, 1994, 1995a, 1995b, 1998; Dill & Boykin, 2000); (b) pedagogical content knowledge (Shulman, 1986,

1987; Grossman, 1990, 1994; Stein & Nelson, 2003); and (c) authentic learning (National Commission on Service Learning, 2002; Newmann, Marks, & Gamoran, 1996; Newmann, 1996; Resnick, 1994).

Some researchers have attempted to quantify the association between principal leadership, on one hand, and student achievement and other school outcomes, on the other. For example, Newmann, Rutter, and Smith (1989) found that measures of principal behaviors can have standardized regression coefficients up to 0.38 on teachers' sense of efficacy, community, and expectation, indicating small effects of principal behaviors. School organizational factors, many of which measure principal behaviors, account for about 10% to 38% of the total variance in teacher efficacy, community, and expectations (Newmann et al., 1989). Later, Barnett, McCormick, and Conners (2000) suggested that school leadership is characterized by a one-to-one relationship between the principal (leader) and the teacher (follower). Under this relationship, teacher-related outcomes (principal leadership and school culture), overall, show an intra-class correlation of up to 25%. Although statistically significant, principal behaviors often show small effects on teacher-related outcomes such as school culture (Barnett et al., 2000). More recently, Marzano, Waters, and McNulty (2005) conducted a landmark meta-analysis of 70 empirical studies published in the last 25 years and found that the simple bivariate correlation between principal leadership and student achievement at the school level, corrected for attenuation, is .25. By definition, then, principal leadership accounts for about 6.25% of the variance in student achievement at the school level. In summary, various effect sizes from the above studies indicate the significant role of principals in improving schools and student achievement.

Seven Important Dimensions of Learning-Centered Principalship

We synthesized the literature on principalship and developed the following seven important dimensions of principalship with a focus on student learning. It is a list that principals could easily recall, identify, and emphasize. We show in Table 1.2 how the seven dimensions of learning-centered leadership are related to the literature including Marzano, Waters, and McNulty's (2005) balanced leadership, ISLLC 2008 standards (Council of Chief State School Officers, 2008), and other elements in research.

Table 1.2 *Principal Leadership Dimensions and Elements Empirically Associated with School Improvement and Student Achievement*

*S1Fb means Standard 1 Function b.

Dimensions	Elements in Marzano's Balanced Leadership	ISLLC Standards 2008	Elements in Other Research
A. Data-informed decision-Making	• Monitor/evaluate • Situational awareness	• Collect and use data to identify goals, assess organizational effectiveness, and promote organizational learning (S1Fb)* • Monitor and evaluate progress and revise plans (S1Fe) • Monitor and evaluate the impact of the instructional program (S2Fi) • Collect and analyze data and information pertinent to the educational environment (S4Fa) • Assess, analyze, and anticipate emerging trends and initiatives in order to adapt leadership strategies (S6Fc)	• Data-informed leadership (Knapp, Swinnerton, Copland, & Monpas-Huber, 2006) • The practice of teachers; student opportunity to learn; academic learning time (Hallinger & Heck, 1996; Shen, Cooley, Reeves, Burt, Rainey, & Yuan, 2010) • Supervising and evaluating the curriculum (Witziers, Bosker, & Kruger, 2003) • Information collection (Celio & Harvey, 2005; Leithwood & Jantzi, 1999; Shen et al., 2010; Wayman & Stringfield, 2006) • Organizational learning (Marks, Louis, & Printy, 2000). • Tools to improve data-informed decision-making for principalship and the school improvement process (Shen, Berry, Cooley, Kirby, Marx, & Whale, 2007; Shen, Cooley, Ma, Reeves, Burt, Rainey, & Yuan, 2012)
B. Safe and orderly school operation	• Order • Communication • Discipline	• Monitor and evaluate the management and operational systems (S3Fa) • Obtain, allocate, align, and efficiently utilize human, fiscal, and technological resources (S3Fb) • Promote and protect the welfare and safety of students and staff (S3Fc)	• Safe and orderly school environment; positive and supportive school climate; communication and interaction; interpersonal support (Cotton, 2003) • Governance (Heck, 1992; Heck & Marcoulides, 1993) • Planning; structure and organization (Leithwood & Jantzi, 1999) • Minimizing classroom disruptions (Sebring & Bryk, 2000)

Dimensions	Elements in Marzano's Balanced Leadership	ISLLC Standards 2008	Elements in Other Research
C. High, cohesive, and culturally relevant expectations for students	• Culture • Focus • Outreach • Ideals/beliefs	• Nurture and sustain a culture of collaboration, trust, learning, and high expectations (S2Fa) • Create a personalized and motivating learning environment for students (S2Fc) • Ensure a system of accountability for every student's academic and social success (S5Fa)	• Goals focused on high levels of student learning; high expectations of students; community outreach (Cotton, 2003) • Climate (Heck, 1992; O'Donnell & White, 2005) • Leadership of parents positively associated with student achievement (Pounder, 1995) • School mission, teacher expectation, school culture (Hallinger & Heck, 1996) • Defining and communicating mission; achievement orientation (O'Donnell & White, 2005; Witziers, Bosker, & Kruger, 2003) • Culture (Leithwood & Jantzi, 1999) • Collective efficacy (Goddard, 2001; Goddard, Hoy, & Hoy, 2004; Manthey, 2006) • Collective responsibility (Lee & Smith, 1996) • Culturally relevant pedagogy (Boykin & Cunningham, 2001; Dill & Boykin, 2000; Ladson-Billings, 1994, 1995a, 1995b, 1998)
D. Distributive and empowering leadership	• Input • Resources • Visibility • Contingent reward • Relationship	• Collaboratively develop and implement a shared vision and mission (S1Fa) • Nurture and sustain a culture of collaboration, trust, learning, and high expectations (S2Fa) • Develop the instructional and leadership capacity of staff (S2Ff) • Develop the capacity for distributed leadership (S3Fd) • Model principles of self-awareness, reflective practice, transparency, and ethical behavior (S5Fb)	• Shared leadership and staff empowerment; visibility and accessibility; teacher autonomy; support for risk taking; professional opportunities and resources (Cotton, 2003) • Cultivating teacher leadership for school improvement; shared instructional leadership (Marks & Printy, 2003) • Promoting school improvement and professional development (Witziers, Bosker, & Kruger, 2003) • Teacher empowerment (Louis & Marks, 1997)

Dimensions	Elements in Marzano's Balanced Leadership	ISLLC Standards 2008	Elements in Other Research
		• Safeguard the values of democracy, equity, and diversity (S5Fc)	• Professional community (Louis, Marks, Kruse, 1996; Marks & Louis, 1997; Spillane, Halverson, & Diamond, 2001) • Social trust (Sebring & Bryk, 2000)
E. Coherent curricular programs	• Curriculum, instruction. assessment • Knowledge of curriculum, instruction, and assessment	• Create a comprehensive, rigorous, and coherent curricular program (S2Fb) • Create a personalized and motivating learning environment for students (S2Fc) • Supervise instruction (S2Fd) • Promote the use of the most effective and appropriate technologies to support teaching and learning (S2Fh) • Maximize time spent on quality instruction (S2Fg) • Ensure teacher and organizational time is focused to support quality instruction and student learning (S3Fe)	• Instructional organization (Hallinger & Heck, 1996; Heck, 1992; Heck & Marcoulides, 1993) • The integration of transformational and shared instructional leadership (Marks & Printy, 2003) • Supervising and evaluating the curriculum; coordinating and managing curriculum (Witziers, Bosker, & Kruger, 2003) • Instructional program coherence (Newmann, Smith, Allensworth, & Bryk, 2001)
F. Real-time and embedded instructional assessment	• Curriculum, instruction, assessment • Knowledge of curriculum, instruction, and assessment	• Develop assessment and accountability systems to monitor student progress (S2Fe) • Monitor and evaluate the impact of the instructional program (S2Fi)	• Instructional leadership; classroom observation and feedback to teachers (Cotton, 2003) • Instructional organization (Hallinger & Heck, 1996; Heck, 1992; Heck & Marcoulides, 1993) • The integration of transformational and shared instructional leadership (Marks & Printy, 2003) • Monitoring student progress (Witziers, Bosker, & Kruger, 2003) • Instructional program coherence (Newmann, Smith, Allensworth, & Bryk, 2001)

Dimensions	Elements in Marzano's Balanced Leadership	ISLLC Standards 2008	Elements in Other Research
G. Passion and commitment for school renewal	• Affirmation • Change agent • Optimizer • Flexibility • Intellectual stimulation	• Collaboratively develop and implement a shared vision and mission (S1F1) • Create and implement plans to achieve goals (S1Fc) • Promote continuous and sustainable improvement (S1Fd) • Promote understanding, appreciation, and use of the community's diverse cultural, social, and intellectual resources (S4Fb) • Build and sustain positive relationships with families and caregivers (S4Fc) • Build and sustain productive relationships with community partners (S4Fd) • Promote social justice and ensure that individual student needs inform all aspects of schooling (S5Fe) • Consider and evaluate the potential moral and legal consequences of decision-making (S5Fd) • Advocate for children, families, and caregivers (S6Fa) • Act to influence local, district, state, and national decisions affecting student learning (S6Fb)	• Self-efficacy (Smith, Guarino, Strom, & Adams, 2006), self-confidence, responsibility, and perseverance; rituals, ceremonies, and other symbolic actions (Cotton, 2003) • Influence of principal leadership on school process such as school policies and norms, the practices of teachers, and school goals (Hallinger & Heck, 1996) • The integration of transformational and shared instructional leadership (Marks & Printy, 2003) • Visibility (Witziers, Bosker, & Kruger, 2003) • Purposes and goals (Leithwood & Jantzi, 1999) • Encouraging teachers to take risks and try new teaching methods (Sebring & Bryk, 2000)

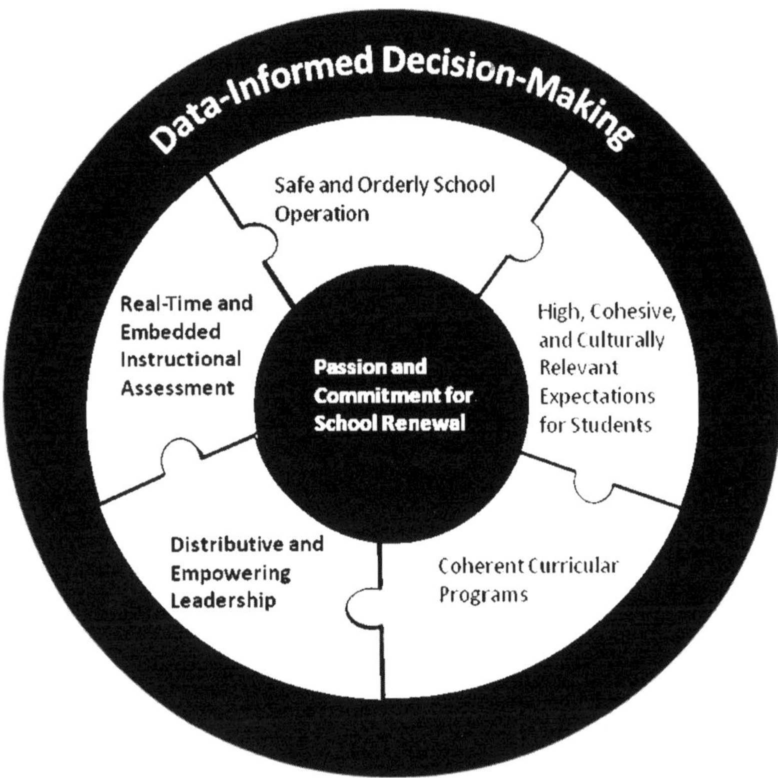

Figure 1.1 Seven Dimensions of Learning-Centered Principalship

School Renewal as Systemic Work

Highlighting the seven important dimensions of principals' work does not mean that principals should practice these seven dimensions separately. The seven dimensions are closely related and school renewal is systemic work. We feel that seven dimensions is a manageable number of dimensions along which principals could intentionally plan their work and reflect upon their experience. "Data-informed decision-making" heads the list because it is foundational to all the other dimensions of principal work. An exposure to the dimension of "data-informed decision-making" will help principals begin to incorporate data into other dimensions of their work. "Passion and commitment for school renewal" is the foundational piece that serves as a capstone for all dimensions. In between these two foundational dimensions, we can discuss more basic ones such as "safe and orderly school climate" and "high, cohesive, and culturally relevant expectations for students." After the dimension of "distributive and empowering leadership," we focus on two important dimensions that are directly related to teaching and learning in school—"coherent curricular programs" and "real-time and embedded instructional assessment." The seven dimensions are literature based, mutually exclusive, and logical guides to principals' work. Figure 1.1 depicts the relationship among the seven dimensions in the school renewal process that form a solid foundation for learning-centered principalship.

The Organization of the Book

Following this introductory chapter, each dimension is the topic of a chapter. Within each chapter, authors first introduce the topic and define key terms as needed. They then engage in a literature review to illustrate the key ideas and research findings in the literature as related to a certain topic. Authors also provide some examples of best practices, resources, and an annotated bibliography. Each chapter establishes a knowledge base on the topic and provides some concrete resources.

Endnote

1 This and the following section include excerpts from Shen, J., Cooley, V., Ma, X., Reeves, P., Burt, W., Rainey, J. M., & Yuan, W. (2012). Data-informed decision-making on high-impact strategies: Developing and validating an instrument for principals. *Journal of Experimental Education,* 80(1), 1–25, published by the Taylor & Francis Group, LLC. The source is acknowledged.

References

Barnett, K., McCormick, J., & Conners, R. (2000, December). *Leadership behaviour of secondary school principals, teacher outcomes and school culture.* Paper presented at the annual conference of the Australian Association for Research in Education. Sydney, Australia.

Beck, L., & Murphy, J. (1993). *Understanding principalship: Metaphorical themes 1920s–1990s.* New York: Teachers College Press.

Bossert, S., Dwyer, D., Rowan, B., & Lee, G. (1982).The instructional management role of the principal. *Educational Administration Quarterly, 18*(3), 34–64.

Boykin, A. W., & Cunningham, R. T. (2001). The effects of movement expressiveness in story content and learning context on the analogical reasoning performance of African American children. *Journal of Negro Education, 70*(1–2), 72–83.

Celio, M. B., & Harvey, J. (2005). *Buried treasure: Developing a management guide from mountains of school data.* New York: Wallace Foundation.

Cooley, V. E., & Shen, J. (2000). Factors influencing applying for urban principalship. *Education and Urban Society, 32*(4), 443–454.

Cooley, V. E., & Shen, J. (2003). School accountability and professional job responsibilities: A perspective from secondary principals. *NASSP Bulletin, 87*(634), 10–25.

Cotton, K. (2003). *Principals and student achievement: What the research says.* Alexandria, VA: Association for Supervision and Curriculum Development.

Council of Chief State School Officers. (2008). *Educational Leadership Policy Standards: ISLLC 2008.* Washington, DC: Author.

Dill, E. M., & Boykin, A.W. (2000). The comparative influence of individual, peer tutoring, and communal learning contexts on the text recall of African American children. *Journal of Black Psychology, 26*(1), 65–78.

Goddard, R. D. (2001). Collective efficacy: A neglected construct in the study of schools and student achievement. *Journal of Educational Psychology*, 93, 467–476.

Goddard, R. D., Hoy, W. K., & Hoy, A. W. (2004). Collective efficacy beliefs: Theoretical developments, empirical evidence, and future directions. *Educational Researcher, 33*(3), 1–13.

Goldring, E., & Pasternak, R. (1994). Principals' coordinating strategies and school effectiveness. *School Effectiveness and School Improvement, 5*(3), 239–253.

Grossman, P. L. (1990). *The making of a teacher: Teacher knowledge and teacher education.* New York: Teachers College Press.

Grossman, P. L. (1994). *Preparing teachers of substance: Prospects for joint work.* Seattle: Occasional Paper No. 20, Center for Educational Renewal, College of Education, University of Washington.

Hallinger, P. (1992). Changing norms of principal leadership in the United States. *Journal of Educational Administration, 30*(3), 35–48.

Hallinger, P., Bickman, L., & Davis, K. (1996). School context, principal leadership, and student reading achievement. *The Elementary School Journal, 96*, 527–549.

Hallinger, P., & Heck, R. H. (1996). Reassessing the principal's role in school effectiveness: A review of empirical research, 1980–1995. *Educational Administration Quarterly, 32*(1), 5–44.

Heck, R. H, & Marcoulides, G. A. (1992). Principal assessment: Conceptual problem, methodological problem, or both? *Peabody Journal of Education, 68*(1), 124–144.

Heck, R. H. (1992). Principals' instructional leadership and school performance: Implications for policy development. *Educational Evaluation and Policy Analysis, 14*(1), 21–34.

Heck, R. H., & Marcoulides, G. A. (1993). Principal leadership behaviors and school achievement. *NASSP Bulletin, 77*(553), 20–28.

Heck, R. H, Larson, T., & Marcoulides, G. A. (1990). Principal instructional leadership and school achievement: Validation of a causal model. *Educational Administration Quarterly, 26,* 94–125.

Knapp, M. S., Swinnerton, J. A., Copland, M. A., & Monpas-Huber, J. (2006). *Data-informed leadership in education.* University of Washington: Center for the Study of Teaching and Policy.

Ladson-Billings, G. (1994). *The dreamkeepers: Successful teachers of African American children.* San Francisco: Jossey-Bass.

Ladson-Billings, G. (1995b). But that's just good teaching? The case for culturally relevant pedagogy. *Theory into Practice, 34,* 159–165.

Ladson-Billings, G. (1995a). Toward a theory of culturally relevant pedagogy. *American Educational Research Journal, 32,* 465–491.

Ladson-Billings, G. (1998). Teaching in dangerous times: Culturally relevant approaches to teacher assessment. *The Journal of Negro Education, 67,* 255–267.

Lee, V., & Smith, J. B. (1996). Collective responsibility for learning and its effects on gains in achievement and engagement for early secondary school students. *American Journal of Education, 104*(2), 103–147.

Leithwood, K. A., & Jantzi, D. (1999). The relative effects of principal and teacher sources of leadership on student engagement with school. *Educational Administration Quarterly, 35* supp, 679–706.

Leithwood, K., Louis, K. S., Anderson, S., & Wahlstrom, K. (2004). *How leadership influences student learning.* Minneapolis: University of Minnesota, Center for Applied Research and Educational Improvement. Retrieved on January 31, 2008 from http://www.wallacefoundation.org/NR/rdonlyres/E3BCCFA5-A88B-45D3–8E27-B973732283C9/0/ReviewofResearchLearningFromLeadership.pdf

Louis, K. S., Marks, H., M. & Kruse, S. D. (1996). Teachers' professional community in restructuring schools. *American Journal of Education, 33*(4), 757–798.

Manthey, G. (2006). Collective efficacy: Explaining school achievement. *Leadership, 35*(3), 23–24.

Marcoulides, G., & Heck, R. (1993). Organizational culture and performance: Proposing and testing a model. *Organization Science, 4*(2), 209–225.

Marks, H. M., & Louis, K. S. (1997). Does teacher empowerment affect the classroom? The implications of teacher empowerment for instructional practice and student academic performance. *Educational Evaluation and Policy Analysis, 19,* 245–275.

Marks, H. M., Louis K. S., & Printy, S. M. (2000). The capacity for organizational learning: Implications for pedagogy and student achievement. In K. Leithwood (Ed.), *Organizational learning and school improvement* (pp. 239–266). Greenwich, CT: JAI.

Marks, H. M., & Printy, S. M. (2003). Principal leadership and school performance: An integration of transformational and instructional leadership. *Educational Administration Quarterly, 39*(3), 370–397.

Marzano, R.J., Waters, T., McNulty, B. A. (2005). *School leadership that works.* Alexandria, VA: Association for Supervision and Curriculum Development.

National Commission on Service Learning. (2002). *Learning in deed: The power of service-learning for American schools.* Newton, MA: Author.

Newmann, F. E., Smith, B., Allensworth, E., & Bryk, A. S. (2001). Instructional program coherence: What it is and why it should guide school improvement policy. *Educational Evaluation and Policy Analysis, 23,* 297–321.

Newmann, F. M.(1996). *Authentic achievement: Restructuring schools for intellectual quality.* San Francisco: Jossey-Bass.

Newmann, F. M., Marks, H. M., & Gamoran, A. (1996). Authentic pedagogy and student performance. *American Journal of Education, 104*(4), 280–312.

Newmann, F. M., Rutter, R. A., & Smith, M. S. (1989). Organizational factors that affect school sense of efficacy, community, and expectations. *Sociology of Education, 62,* 221–238.

O'Donnell, R. J, & White, G. P. (2005). Within the accountability era: Principal instructional leadership behaviors and student achievement. *NASSP Bulletin, 89*(645), 56–-72.

Portin, B. S., & Shen, J. (2005).The changing principalship. In J., Shen, et al., *School Leadership* (pp. 179–199). New York: Peter Lang.

Portin, B., Shen, J., & Williams, R. (1998). The changing principalship and its impact: Voices from principals. *NASSP Bulletin, 82*(602), 1–8.

Pounder, D. G. (1995). Leadership as an organization-wide phenomenon: Its impact on school performance. *Educational Administration Quarterly, 31*(4), 564–588.

Resnick, L. B. (1994). Performance puzzles: Using assessments as a means of defining standards. *American Journal of Education, 102,* 511–526.

Rodriguez-Campo, L., Rincones-Gomez, R., & Shen, J. (2005). Secondary principals' educational attainment, experience, and professional development. *International Journal of Leadership in Education, 8*(4), 309–319.

Sebring, B., & Bryk, A. (2000). School leadership and the bottom line in Chicago. *Phi Delta Kappan, 81,* 440–443.

Shen, J., Berry, J., Cooley, V., Kirby, B., Marx, G., & Whale, D. (2007). *Data-informed decision-making: A guidebook for data points and analyses in the context of Michigan School Improvement Framework.* Kalamazoo, MI: Michigan Coalition of Educational Leadership.(www.wmich.edu/wallacegrant/docs/DIDM.pdf)

Shen, J., Cooley, V., Ma, X., Reeves, P., Burt, W., Rainey, J. M., & Yuan, W. (2012). Data-informed decision-making on high-impact strategies: Developing and validating an instrument for principals. *Journal of Experimental Education,* 80(1), 1–25.

Shen, J., Cooley, V., Reeves, P., Burt, W., Ryan, L., Rainey, J. M., & Yuan, W. (2010). Using data for decision-making: Perspectives from 16 principals in Michigan, USA. *International Review of Education, 56*, 435–456.

Shen, J., Cooley, V., & Wegenke, G. (2004). Perspectives on factors influencing application of principalship: A comparative study of teachers, principals, and superintendents. *International Journal of Leadership in Education, 7*(1), 57–70.

Shen, J., & Crawford, C. S. (2003). The characteristic of the secondary principalship: An introduction to the special issue. *NASSP Bulletin, 87*(634), 2–8.

Shen, J., Kavanaugh, A., Wegenke, G., Rodriguez-Campos, L., Rincones-Gomez, R., Palmer, L. B., Crawford, C., Cooley, V. E., Poppink, S., VanderJagt, D., Hsieh, C., Ruhl-Smith, C. D., Keiser, N. M., & Portin, B. (2005). *School principals.* New York: Peter Lang.

Shulman, L. S. (1986). Those who understand: Knowledge growth in teaching. *Educational Researcher, 15*, 4–14.

Shulman, L. S. (1987). Knowledge and teaching: Foundations of the new reform. *Harvard Educational Review, 57*(1), 1–22.

Smith, W., Guarino, A., Strom, P., & Adams, O. (2006). Effective teaching and learning environments and principal self-efficacy. *Journal of Research for Educational Leaders, 3*(2), 4–23.

Spillane, J. P., Halverson, R., & Diamond, J. B. (2001).Investigating school leadership practice: A distributed perspective. *Educational Researcher, 30*(3), 23–28.

Stein, M. K., & Nelson, B. S. (2003). Leadership content knowledge. *Educational Evaluation and Policy Analysis, 25*(4), 423–448.

Wayman, J. C., & Stringfield, S. (2006). Technology-supported involvement of entire faculties in examination of student data for instructional improvement. *American Journal of Education, 112*, 549–571.

Weiss, R. S. (1992). *Elementary school principals: An historical evolution.* Amherst, MA: University of Massachusetts at Amherst Press.

Witziers, B., Bosker, R. J., & Kruger, M. L. (2003). Educational leadership and student achievement: The elusive search for an association. *Educational Administration Quarterly, 39*(3), 398–425.

2

Data-Informed Decision-Making

VAN E. COOLEY AND JIANPING SHEN

Introduction

Business and industrial leaders and other professionals have used data to monitor performance, product quality, and programmatic outcomes for decades. Borman (2002) described the evolution of assessment in agriculture, technology, and medicine, suggesting that in medicine, clinical trials in polio and research on coronary disease and other conditions have saved lives and improved the conditions of society. Criticisms of the failure of high school graduates to perform in the workplace, political pressures, and the reality of a world marketplace have created awareness that changes in education are necessary. Convergence of political and economic factors with the perspective that schools have failed has made education ripe for assessment and accountability, much as what has transpired in other professions. From a policy perspective, the driving force for educational change is No Child Left Behind (NCLB). NCLB established reporting and accountability standards for schools, districts, and state education agencies as states must identify adequate yearly progress objectives and disaggregate data by student subgroups (Jackson & Lunenburg, 2010). Teachers and administrators are now held accountable for student learning, which has resulted in a greater reliance on data for assessment. Although not explicitly stated in NCLB, it is implied that data should be used to inform and initiate change (Wayman, 2005). Legislation does not automatically translate into compliance, and even with federal and state mandates establishing uniform data collection and reporting requirements, differences in scope, depth, and breadth of data collected, district analytical procedures, and the fiscal and technical support provided to teachers and administrators have varied as widely as gaps in student achievement.

The focus on accountability has resulted in considerable tension, finger pointing, and diminished communication among principals, teachers, and central office administrators. One principal described communication between central office and building administrators as a "shell game" where principals meet with central office staff and merely nod, often acquiescing with limited honest discussion (Shen & Cooley, 2008). The challenge is that central office administrators, principals, and teachers visualize data through different lenses. Central office administrators view data from standardized test scores and how the district compares to neighboring districts; whereas, teachers and principals see data as a tool to improve student learning. Aside from the diverse perspectives, the reality is teachers, principals, and superintendents face enormous pressure to increase student achievement with attention now placed on the classroom and student performance with standardized tests.

The standards-based reform movement has resulted in major changes in teacher and administrator roles in that educators must use data to quantify student learning (Moss & Piety, 2007). Teachers find themselves in the "eye of the storm" with many outside voices challenging their competence. They respond with anger and dissatisfaction, emphasizing that what they do in a classroom cannot be accurately measured. Although the complexities of teaching and differences in students are acknowledged, a long-standing body of research suggests steps teachers can take to increase student achievement (Marzano, 2003). For example, Chubb and Moe (1990) found that students in effective high schools achieved at least a half year more in their late two years of school than their counterparts in ineffective high schools. Marzano (2003) reported that students with the most effective teachers gained more than 53% compared to 14% with the least effective teachers. Over a three-year period, Haycock (1998) reported an 83% gain in classrooms with effective teachers compared to a 29% increase with the least effective teachers. Some teachers are simply more effective than others, a fact that is often ignored.

The age-old excuse that some students cannot learn is no longer a viable argument. Effective teachers make adjustments in instruction when students do not learn. Teaching is commensurate with problem solving and understanding why students are learning and why students are not learning. NCLB holds administrators accountable for student learning with processes now in place to remove principals in schools that fail to achieve. In addition, a school may be reconstituted if it repeatedly fails to meet adequate yearly progress standards.

Data-driven, Data-based, or Data-informed?

There is an ongoing debate about the role of data in the decision-making process. A common language and understanding are critical to the way that data are used in the school improvement process. The critical question is, "Are decisions datadriven, databased, or datainformed?" It must be recognized data are not a panacea for all educational problems and challenges. Second, principals must understand the complexity of the argument and be cognizant that behind the numbers and reports are student faces, parental support, and the many diverse challenges that children bring to school. And finally, leaders must realize that high-stakes standardized tests fail to elicit all the information required to analyze the complexities of the learning process. Knapp and his colleagues (2007) contend data should inform rather than drive decisions. Other elements and factors must be considered in order to understand the teaching and learning process. However, data provide a sound foundation that influences effective decision-making in a number of program areas. Data-informed decision-making is not in practice a direct action-reaction response but is complicated and impacted by core values, perspectives, and previously formed opinions. Leaders must use data carefully to generate questions in order to interpret standardized test results correctly. Through responses to comments and inquiries, data provide information for teachers and school leaders to develop strategies that impact student learning (Knapp, Copland, & Swinnerton, 2007).

Although data-driven decision-making is still the dominant term in the literature, we will use the term "data-informed decision-making" in the following. If the original sources used "data-informed," we will keep it to remain true to the original sources. However, we maintain that data must inform, rather than drive, decisions in order to be used effectively.

The Role of Inquiry in Data-informed Decision-making

Data provide a glimpse of how students are performing at a particular date and time. Data must propagate continuous inquiry and not just answer the question of the day (Earl & Katz, 2006). Inquiry and looking beyond the numbers to transform data into useful information for instructional adjustments are important. For example, most of us understand that on occasion a teacher may be assigned a group of students who struggle with basic concepts. Another group of teachers might have a large numbers of students transferring from other districts or significant numbers of second-language or special needs students. The process is not about finding excuses but determining why students fail to meet district standards and using data to design and implement strategies that address learning deficiencies. Leaders must recognize that data-informed decision-making is a time-consuming process, which will, however, help avoid misguided assumptions about student achievement. To make appropriate decisions about program effectiveness, data must be analyzed over a period of years, disaggregated, and examined across class sections and teachers using multiple sources (Bernhardt, 1998). Only a systematic process of data analysis can develop questions and inform decisions. What emerges from a comprehensive analysis is a more complete portrait of the learning process focusing on a number of interrelated concepts that provide valuable information on teaching, program effectiveness, student sociological and demographic factors, and the overall learning process.

Most of the literature addresses data-informed decision-making based on normative arguments, but only a small amount of that literature is based on empirical studies. Research on the impact of data-informed decision-making on student achievement is essentially non-existent. Researchers and educators continue to debate the challenges of measuring student performance. The problem is accentuated by student diversity, the problems students bring to school, peer influences, the students' family background, socioeconomic status, neighborhood influences, and home environment. Data-informed decision-making in education is a relative new area, and a number of new methodologies will assist in measuring teacher and student performance. Most current research focuses on strategies to strengthen the data analysis process. The following section summarizes major themes from the literature on data-informed decision-making.

Types of Data and Data Intersection

A wide range of data is used in the decision-making. According to Dahlkemper (2002), data can be categorized as either *qualitative* or *quantitative.* Qualitative data tend to focus on measures such as observations, focus groups, and examination of student products, student recitation, and other classroom work. For quantitative data, emphasis is on factors such as standardized test results, student and teacher absenteeism, and the amount of time spent on instruction. Both types of data may be used for (a) diagnosis and clarification, (b) exploring alternatives, (c) justification for strategies or actions, (d) compliance, (e) guiding practice, and (f) a management tool to determine how the organization is doing (Knapp, Copland, & Swinnerton, 2007). Teacher and administrator data use varies, being typically limited to analyzing standardized test scores (Shen, Cooley, Reeves, Burt, Ryan, Rainey, & Yuan, 2010). Most current teacher and administrator data use is related to compliance rather than inquiry, which means that careful analysis and linking of data to student learning seldom occur. Effective data use is related to teacher and administrator expertise, and most educators lack training and knowledge in data analysis. Professional development must inculcate data-informed decision-making into the teacher or administrator's daily activities. The ability to use data to inform curriculum and instructional decisions represents a major shift in teacher and administrator job actions.

Data can be *static* or *real time.* There are a number of disadvantages to static data (data three to five months old). Educators often receive standardized test results at the conclusion of the school year, and the time lapse between testing and the return of test results makes meaningful modifications in curriculum and instruction difficult. Teachers and administrators leave for summer recess with test results buried in a file that may never be revisited. Although standardized test results could be shared with teachers in the next grade level, in most instances, this does not actually occur.

Data can also be classified as *formative* or *summative.* The limitations of standardized tests have caused educators to explore formative measures that can provide teachers with more current information on classroom practice and student learning. Real-time formative data include teacher-developed tests, student homework, writing assignments, demonstrations, etc. Formative data do not meet the criteria outlined in NCLB as they are not outcome measures, but they have merit and can support learning and the data-analysis process. Popham (2008) described formative assessment as a series of adjustments made when students fail to learn a particular concept. Formative assessments provide teachers with information for daily changes and adjustments in teaching, instructional practices, materials, and assignments. Halverson (2010) developed a formative assessment model that included interventions, assessments, and actuation that informs instruction. Interventions can be comprised of instructional strategies, materials, use of technology, student-writing assignments in the form of classwork, and homework. Informal assessments supply timely feedback on learning and mastery of concepts. In this cyclical process, teachers can make ongoing instructional adjustments.

Business leaders originally used benchmarking as a methodology to monitor and compare the productivity of competitors. The concept is related to Deming's early work in systems thinking and is closely aligned with the quality improvement movement (Bounds, Dobbins, & Fowler, 1995). Benchmarking in education has emerged as an important component of the assessment processes, providing foundational information to effectively monitor student progress. According to Grayson (2006), the benchmarking process identifies causative factors in relation to change and improvements. This systematic perspective (a) examines: process maps or the overall work and steps that need to be completed to meet goals; (b) process measures that provide time-sensitive quantitative measures of progress in meeting targets; (c) process comparisons that supply information within a school or district or with schools in other districts; (d) process improvement that reflects ongoing incremental improvement; and (e) process innovation that involves redesign, modification, new processes and methodologies, and modifications of goals. Benchmarking data and performance, programs, and processes allow leaders to move beyond intuition focusing on information and multiple areas that may need to be addressed.

Benchmarking is most often equated with student progress on standardized tests. Alignment of student performance on formative assessments and state tests provides benchmarks to make curriculum and instructional changes that impact student learning. Benchmarking must move beyond standardized test scores and include all factors that impact student achievement. Leaders must resist focusing on symptoms and examine interconnected causes that impact student learning. Benchmarks should connect formative and summative assessments that provide information to drive the school improvement process. Above all, benchmarking is both a short-term and longitudinal improvement tool designed to provide leaders with information on a wide range of areas to establish improvement strategies.

There are limitations and shortcomings in formative assessment (Ericsson, 2007). In addition to collecting data and examining student projects, teachers must not only understand and decipher information but should also be able to develop new instructional strategies to address identified shortcomings and areas of need. Formative assessment may be compromised by district mandates to use pacing guides which limit the teacher's ability to re-teach concepts instead of moving ahead and thus allowing students to fall through the cracks. Black and Wiliam (1998) reviewed 250 articles and books, concluding that formative assessment produced significant gains in student achievement impacting at-risk students and students with disabilities more than other students. Formative assessment helps teachers identify gaps in the learning process (Ramaprasad, 1983; Sadler, 1989). Formative assessments complement standardized tests, and when these assessments are closely aligned with standardized tests, the inquiry process and modifications to address gaps in student learning are strengthened.

Bernhardt (1998, 2004, 2010) was one of the first to promote viewing data through multiple lenses. Data intersections serve as a roadmap to systematically examine data. Each of the four data streams—student learning or achievement data, demographic data, perceptual data, and school process data—provides useful informational tools for teachers and administrators to intervene and develop learning strategies. Student learning or achievement data include standardized tests, criterion reference tests, and district- and vendor-developed formative assessments. Demographic data focus on gender, socioeconomic status, and other student-, family-, or community-related data. Perceptual data include teacher values and beliefs about a student's capacity to learn and school and community perspectives on the educational process. Perceptions impact both teacher and student performance. This is especially true when examining student self-esteem issues, and whether teachers and administrators feel that students are capable of learning. Some teachers will not assign homework because they believe students will not do it. Others will not allow students to take books and materials outside the classroom, because they feel students will lose or misplace the materials. What is the impact of these actions on student growth and development and the overall learning process? Examining such beliefs and perceptions is part of the data analysis process.

Processes are the areas in which educators can make significant changes that may directly impact student learning. Bernhardt (2004) categorized process data into district-level process, school-level processes, and classroom-level processes. District processes include programs, policies, student grouping, teacher assignments, professional development, and support structures for students. School processes include scheduling, teacher factors including teacher quality and teaching behaviors, support personnel, school discipline, and attendance policies. Instructional strategies, homework assignments, classroom assessments, student grouping, remediation, and skill-building strategies are examples of classroom practices. Educators must generate questions and carefully examine processes at each of the three levels and formulate questions that help measure the impact of programs on student learning. Are programs meeting student needs? Are teachers following the district curriculum? How many days are teachers and students absent? Reviewing processes at the district, school, and classroom levels are often overlooked. Factors at each process level impact student performance.

Data intersections help teachers and principals to connect student faces and programs to data. Through data intersections, educators examine programs, procedures, curriculum, instruction, sociological factors, support programming, and other influences that impact learning. Disaggregating data involves ongoing analysis of each of the four data streams and the impact of each data stream on student achievement. Reviewing student achievement on standardized tests will not lead to increased student achievement without connecting multiple data dimensions with why students are learning or not learning.

Kowalski, Lasley, and Mahoney (2008) identified four phases for connecting data to school improvement. These phases are closely connected to Bernhardt's data intersections and include collecting, connecting, creating, and confirming. Teachers, principals, and school officials are bombarded with data. Decisions need to be made on what data are to be collected. Once data are collected, the data must be connected, such as connecting the formative and summative data or looking at data through multiple lenses. Creating is the problem-solving action phase in which gaps are identified and goals are set. The six steps in the process are (1) defining the problem, (2) discussing assumptions about student learning, (3) validating perceptions of student achievement with data, (4) involving teachers and stakeholders and examining multiple data sources, (5) exploring the utility of current practices, and (6) developing a plan of action. Kowlaski et al.'s creating phase presents a framework for data analysis and making program modifications to address shortcomings in student learning. This phase is often adversely affected by time constraints, contractual issues, teacher and administrator knowledge gaps, and limited cohesion between the district curriculum and the taught curriculum. Confirming, the final phase, involves assessment, evaluation, and validating the process's success. This process is actually far more complex than this review indicates as these actions involve teacher and administrator readiness, changes in the school culture, and other related factors such as time, commitment, and attitudes.

Empirical Research on the Status of Data-Informed Decision-Making

There has been limited empirical research on the effects of data-informed decision-making on student learning. Most research has focused on steps to implement practices that support teacher and administrator data use. The studies cited below represent a sampling of what has been learned about implementing a data-informed decision-making system.

Ikemoto and Marsh's Survey Study (2007). Ikemoto and Marsh (2007) collected data relating to data-driven decision-making practices from educators in 10 districts in four states. The educators involved were 130 district leaders, 100 principals, and 80 other school leaders. The majority of the teachers claimed they frequently used data to analyze student achievement and that district administrators held them accountable for their instructional decisions. Although the survey results did not address student learning, the information collected provides recommendations on what leaders can do to increase and improve teacher and administrator data use. The findings should be viewed from a systems perspective with the understanding that implementing only one or two areas may reduce the effectiveness of the entire data analysis process. The researchers found that: (a) the timely access to data increased teacher use; (b)teachers questioned the validity of standardized tests and noted that results were not representative of student learning; (c) formative assessments and multiple indicators in data analysis helped alleviate teachers' validity concerns (Keeney, 1998; Koretz, 2003; Supovitz & Klein, 2003); (d) many teachers and administrators were unable to effectively analyze data, formulate critical questions, and develop strategies (Choppin, 2002; Mason, 2002); (e) time was required to analyze data; (f) technical assistance, data analysis, and management tools increased data use; and (g) data use was enhanced by open and frank teacher-administrator discussions.

The RAND Corporation Study. The RAND Corporation report on data-informed decision-making by Marsh, Pane, and Hamilton (2006) found that achievement data in the form of state standardized tests were used most often. Value-added modeling (VAM) accounted for such factors as student background, ethnicity, and socioeconomic status and was used in conjunction with standardized tests. Test results were returned late in the school year so teachers and principals had little time to thoroughly analyze the data. Many districts developed and administered local tests that focused on mathematics and reading in the form of item banks aligned with state standards. Teachers were more positive about formative tests and reported that these informal instruments provided information to assess learning and allowed the time to develop strategies to address student weaknesses prior to the conclusion of the school year. School officials used attendance and mobility data and graduation rates but, in general, did not use school process data or data related to classroom effectiveness.

Teachers and superintendents used data for different purposes. Teachers used test scores to establish goals and learning outcomes, and superintendents used data to identify areas of improvement and develop school improvement plans (SIP). Officials in all districts disaggregated test results to identify students who needed additional assistance. More than 75% of principals in three states indicated tests were used to identify "bubble kids" or students close to the state minimum standard. States with a long history of accountability were more likely to promote data-driven decision-making while providing measures to local districts.

Shen, Cooley and Colleagues' Study in Michigan. Shen, Cooley and colleagues (2010) interviewed 16 urban principals about their data use. Student achievement data in the form of standardized tests were used by all 16 principals mainly in the context of accountability. Six of them mentioned using data for school improvement. They also used the data from state standardized tests to determine gaps in student knowledge. Data were discussed at staff meetings and incorporated into school improvement plans. Only two principals used student and community background data. Three principals used process data related to attendance and discipline. None of the principals reported using process data for program and instructional improvement or for teacher assessment. Data use was limited to achievement data, so a more sophisticated analysis using data intersection was essentially nonexistent. Principals revealed that they used data in determining student program eligibility (Title 1), grouping students by achievement level, identifying and placing students in special programs, and deciding the type and amount of services to provide. Achievement data helped identify student strengths and shortcomings. Overall, only one of the 16 principals used disaggregated data even though this was a NCLB requirement. The principals' use of data and overall knowledge of data-informed decision-making was limited.

Practices That Support Data Use in Urban High Schools. Lachat and Smith (2005) conducted research in five urban high schools in three districts. They found that data disaggregation increased teacher and administrator use of data. However, data were not always accessible in a timely fashion. Teacher comfort increased when they worked in teams. The development of questions related to student achievement helped with disaggregation and in establishing improvement strategies. Teacher collaboration and timely, accessible data resulted in the modification of instructional practices, which led to increased student achievement.

New York City Department of Education Study. In 2004, the New York City Department of Education in conjunction with the Grow Network implemented a statewide system of data analysis. The project involved grades 3–8 and used standardized test data and support resources in conjunction with professional development. Reports were generated by school, classroom, subject, and student. An online system allowed teachers to further analyze data. A research project was conducted to determine the impact of the system on administrators and teachers. The data enabled administrators to identify needs, use resources more effectively, identify teachers and students who needed additional support, and establish instructional targets. Reports also increased communication on curriculum, instruction, and steps necessary to meet students' needs and served as a basis for targeted professional development. Teachers used data to identify instructional priorities and develop short- and long-term instructional plans. Teachers also acknowledged that data use allowed them to focus on diverse student needs and increased their awareness of student readiness. Similar to their role in administrator feedback, data reports increased communication among teachers and also served as a basis for providing professional development. Finally, sharing data with students allowed students to assume responsibility for learning.

SchoolNet Instructional System. The School District of Philadelphia implemented a SchoolNet Instructional System which gave teachers the tools to connect a system-wide curriculum to online benchmark testing and data-driven decision-making through desktop accessible data. According to a 2006 study of Philadelphia middle schools, schools with access to technology-enabled intervention experienced positive increases in student achievement in reading, language arts, and mathematics. The system included an instructional management system aligned with district curriculum and benchmarking, with teachers given access to student data. Although researchers cautioned that other district reforms might have impacted the rise in student test scores, their follow-up interviews did not elicit information to minimize SchoolNET's effects on student achievement gains (Brown & Lemke, 2007).

The Impact of Data-Informed Decision-Making

Data-informed decision-making is a complex and relatively new activity for teachers and administrators. Research is limited although a growing body of information indicates that using data to inform instruction positively impacts student achievement. A number of related studies have revealed that teacher data use is positively related to student achievement measures (Edmonds, 1979; Stringfield, 1994; Reynolds & Teddlie, 2000). Data use also impacts on school improvement teams (Chrispeels, Brown, & Castillo, 2000), and there is evidence that teacher and administrator data use helps to develop a more professional culture (Feldman & Tung, 2001). The collaborative use of data also encouraged interdepartmental collaboration in high schools as teachers were able to identify data patterns throughout the entire school. New technologies help to develop systems that increase teacher and administrator data use. Available systems include (a) student information systems (SIS); (b) assessment systems; and, (c) data warehousing systems, each of the three types of systems having both strengths and weaknesses. SIS systems provide attendance and scheduling information and are often limited to the current school year; whereas assessment systems allow educators to organize and analyze data by looking at benchmarks; and data warehouses provide longitudinal data over multiple years (Wayman, 2005).

As to the effect on student achievement, Marzano, Waters, and McNulty (2005) conducted meta-analyses and estimated that principals' "monitoring/evaluating," a leadership responsibility that resembles data-informed decision-making, has a correlation coefficient of 0.25 with student achievement. Shen, Cooley and colleagues (2010) found that for the 8 elementary school principals in a data-informed decision-making project between 2005 and 2008, their schools' Michigan Educational Assessment Program (MEAP) proficiency rate for mathematics and reading increased by 12 percentage points, while the state average only increased by 8 percentage points.

Cook (2001) found limited evidence of the effectiveness of virtually all educational initiatives. Although the literature on data-informed decision-making continues to proliferate, most is normative in nature. In *Using Student Achievement Data to Support Instructional Decision Making* (Hamilton, Halverson, Jackson, Mandinach, Supovitz, & Wayman, 2009), IES developed a rating system to rate research for practice guides. IES offers five recommendations that serve as an important guide to leaders through the data-informed decision-making process:

1. Make data part of an ongoing cycle of instructional improvement;
2. Teach students to examine their own data and set learning goals;
3. Establish a clear vision for school-wide data use;
4. Provide supports that foster a data-driven culture within the school; and
5. Develop and maintain a district-wide data system.

Barriers, Opportunities, and Changes Needed

Our public education system faces a number of factors that inhibit data-informed decision-making. Barriers to data-informed decision-making are complex and in many ways are microcosms of many problems that impact schools. Barriers can be categorized into two distinct, but interrelated, areas. The first category focuses on human factors. These include the knowledge gap, resistance to change, absence of common purpose, and the failure to engage teachers in the accountability process.

Principals and teachers have little or no training in data analysis as universities only recently began to include data-informed decision-making as part of teacher education and administrative preparation curriculum (Shen & Cooley,

2008). This has created a huge challenge for principals who must now analyze data and make decisions without the requisite knowledge. Most principals continue to work with data in limited ways to conform to state and national standards.

The examination of large amounts of data thwarts the data analysis process. In addition, teachers do not have a common understanding, nor are they in agreement on how data should be used. Teachers require professional development and time to develop skills in the data analysis process. Other barriers are the teachers' concept of their role, the individual school and district culture, and beliefs about and experiences with reform (Van Barneveld, 2008).

Related to the knowledge gap is a tendency to embrace the status quo. Educators have been bombarded with reform initiatives over their careers and many see data-informed decision-making as another item in the long line of reforms that come and go. Absence of common purpose represents a more daunting challenge for educational leaders. Central office administrators, teachers, and principals use data for different purposes. Teachers and administrators use data to guide student achievement whereas central office administrators use data to verify compliance with NCLB and report student progress to the board and community. The lack of a common purpose also impacts resources allocated to schools for data analysis, for example, data warehousing systems, targeted professional development, and structural changes that allow teachers and administrators time for data analysis.

Reeves (2010) identified four barriers—a toxic hierarchy, lack of compliance orientation, resistance to change, and a lack of the respect that should be accorded to teachers—that hamper teacher leadership and contribute to organizational ineffectiveness. These factors are pertinent because teachers play a pivotal role in using data to inform instruction. In data-informed decision-making, open communication is key to the effective data use, and central office administrators, principals, and teachers must establish a common purpose for using data. In terms of data-informed decision-making, "compliance to what" is the issue. Compliance to NCLB and state mandates is non-negotiable, but enhanced communication on all levels and a mutual understanding of compliance will strengthen data use. The issue of the lack of respect given to teachers and principals must be addressed. This organizational problem is exacerbated by hierarchical top-down leadership practices. Many teachers have been conditioned to accept rather than participate in educational initiatives. Principals and teachers must be part of the problem-solving process.

Another group of barriers is related to curriculum and instruction issues, organizational issues, resource allocation, and time. In order for schools to analyze and effectively use data, there has to be a common curriculum. Teachers and administrators must reconcile differences in the written curriculum, the taught curriculum, and the assessed curriculum. Teachers and administrators should engage in spirited conversations about what students need to know and be able to do and above all, the curriculum must be followed. Without common standards, it is difficult, if not impossible, to identify gaps in student learning.

Other barriers are related to structures that impact data use. These include time, data access and storage, and targeted professional development. The organizational structure of schools is not conducive to collaborative problem solving. The teacher day is fixed with little time for collaborative problem solving, targeted professional development, or time for data analysis. The teacher's day is consumed with teaching, student assessment, and supervision. In some states, teacher contracts limit the amount of time teachers can meet after regular school hours. Given this limitation, the question remains as to how efficient problem-solving activities are at the end of the school day.

Districts that want to promote data use need to develop and create infrastructures that support data analysis such as software and data warehousing programs where teachers have access to a wide range of data. In conjunction with standardization of curriculum, principals and teachers must develop formative measures that are connected to state standardized tests. Although the state standardized test may drive instruction, in the era of high stakes accountability, concepts on the test must be addressed. Determining what students know and do not know must become part of the formative assessment process.

Finally, the teacher evaluation process is in need of major revision. Assessment must go beyond test scores to include questions as to how data are informing teacher decisions on teaching, instruction, and student learning. Data should be used as part of the teacher evaluation process, but leaders should proceed with caution in using these data to evaluate performance and examine patterns, trends, and student achievement over a period of years. Many background variables should be taken into account and a value-added model should be employed.

A Model of Data-Informed Decision-Making for School Improvement

School officials desiring to use data as a basis for school improvement are advised to consider a comprehensive feedback model that connects personnel, curriculum, and formative and summative assessment with data analysis and improvement processes. Organizational structures designed to engage teachers are also critical to the implementation, nurturing, and enculturation of data-informed decision-making into improvement activities. Figure 2.1 presents a comprehensive model for making data-informed decisions. The Data Feedback Model is based, in part, on the work of a number of experts including Bolman and Deal (2003), Bernhardt (1998, 2004, 2010), Halverson (2010), Popham (2008), and Senge (1990). The model provides principals, teachers, and school leaders a framework to effectively analyze data through multiple lenses that include examination of district curriculum. The model consists of seven interconnected components: (1) data teams, (2) common purpose, (3) articulation of horizontal and vertical curriculum, (4) formative and summative assessment alignment to state standards, (5) data intersection analysis, (6) inquiry to establish strengths and shortcomings, and (7) actions to address areas of need. We will discuss each of the components as follows.

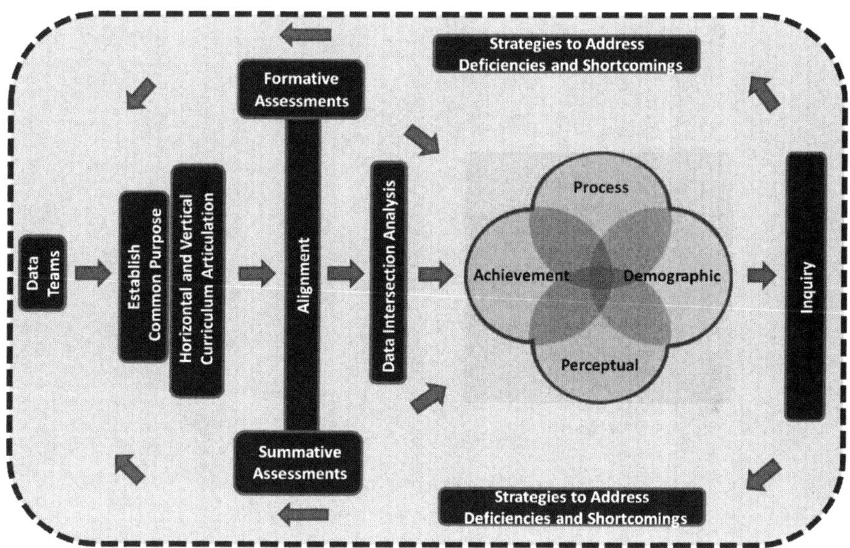

Figure 2.1 Data Feedback Model

*The idea of data intersection (the four intersecting circles in the above figure) was adapted, with permission, from Bernhardt (2004). The permission is acknowledged.

Data Teams

Data teams consist of the principal and teachers representing all disciplines that meet regularly to review data, discuss curriculum and instruction, and issues related to teaching and learning. Team members consist of teachers who are supportive and not resistant of school improvement efforts. Establishing structures where team roles and expectations are agreed to and understood is a critical part of the process. We suggest the team roles be posted so that team members are constantly reminded of their responsibilities. A regular meeting schedule, along with an agenda, timelines for completing work, and published minutes, provides structure in completing tasks and communicating accomplishments to faculty and staff. Team members are encouraged to engage in problem solving in a non-threatening environment that engenders trust and spirited dialogue.

Data teams identify typologies of data that need to be reviewed and analyzed with team members, connecting data with school improvement initiatives, providing feedback on establishing data warehousing systems, professional development for teachers, and other support needed to make data part of the school culture. Data teams also provide recommendations on formative assessment, lead faculty discussions related to student performance, and assume a major leadership role in the data analysis process.

Common Purpose

Data teams must establish a common purpose, which means team members must understand the need for action, and teachers and administrators must know and support why actions are taken. Arriving at a common purpose is an art and a science and takes time, patience, and perseverance. Improved student achievement is certainly at the forefront of the reform movements. There are ramifications for teachers and administrators when students do not learn. Fairly or unfairly, these ramifications can be used as a motivator to promote change and to establish common purpose. A common purpose helps to remove barriers and obstacles and to establish structures and programs to increase student achievement. The common purpose should be simple, easy to understand, and not open to interpretation. Internal marketing of the common purpose is an important step. All teachers and administrators must know and understand why actions need to be taken. A common purpose does not occur by happenstance. Organizational conditions impact the common purpose. When there is a crisis or a problem, establishment of a common purpose becomes even more important. Common purpose is closely related to systems thinking in that teachers and administrators must see patterns, interrelationships, and the reasons for change. Establishing common purpose is a critical step in the data feedback model.

Curriculum Articulation

Once the classroom door closes, there is limited coordination as to what is being taught. Many teachers teach to their strength and often ignore the district curriculum. In other cases, the district may not have an articulated curriculum aligned to state standards. It is crucial that teachers and administrators align the curriculum in the building and between buildings. In a district without an articulated curriculum, data analysis is negated: How can data be analyzed and modifications made if teachers are not following a common curriculum? Can teachers and administrators determine if the problem is with the curriculum, the instruction, or a combination of other factors? The fact that many districts are still struggling to establish a district curriculum is alarming. At both the building and the district level, curriculum alignment is a critical building block to the data-analysis process.

Formative and Summative Assessment Alignment

Formative and summative assessments should be aligned to the district curriculum. Data teams play a pivotal role in alignment of the district curriculum to the formative and summative assessments and state standards. All teachers must be engaged in the process. Once a process is developed, data team members should lead subcommittees that include the entire teaching staff throughout the alignment process. This new and challenging role for teachers requires targeted professional development, nurturing, and ongoing follow-up if the process is to be successful. Many teachers will react with frustration as they have not been trained to be problem solvers. Data team members must stress that teachers must act as problem-solvers and that curriculum development and alignment are required if the problem-solving process is to be successful. Principal leadership and support of data teams are critical: if the principal is not involved and does not support the work of data teams, the process will fail.

Teachers often express concern over standardized test validity and the fact standardized test results are often not returned until the school year concludes. A system in which teachers use formative assessment in conjunction with summative assessment provides real time data that teachers can use to make the critical decisions that impact student learning.

Data Intersection Analysis

Data intersections, as based on the work of Victoria Bernhardt, use achievement data, demographic data, process data, and perceptual data to represent the best opportunity to understand the nuances of student learning. School improvement teams must look at both formative and summative data through multiple lenses to determine strengths and shortcomings. Data analysis is a time-consuming process necessary for teachers and principals to understand the multi-faceted dimensions of student performance. In most districts, teachers and administrators examine achievement data but pay little or no attention to demographics, perceptual, or process data. The result is an incomplete analysis, with little or no attention given to learning obstacles. Is the problem curriculum, instruction, student attendance, a second language, school polices, and programs? The data-intersection analysis process transforms and elevates the role of the teacher and principal.

Inquiry

This step involves reviewing all data (information) and determining what additional questions need to be asked. Program modifications must be based on data. Data teams again play a pivotal role, but all teachers must be involved in the process. We recommend a workshop setting where all teachers play a role in the inquiry process. Data should be posted on butcher paper or projected screens with teachers and administrators asking questions, looking for connections, and engaging in spirited discussion.

Developing Strategies

The final step is developing strategies to address areas of need. Data teams again assume a key role in the process. Table 2.1 provides an example of a data planning matrix that will guide data teams and other members through the process. The matrix consists of eight steps designed to stimulate discussion, action, and accountability.

Table 2.1 Data Planning Matrix

Areas of Strength	Areas of Concern	Data Source	Current Practices New Strategies	Timeline	Roles/ Responsibilities	Assessment Criteria	Required Resources

It is important to focus on strengths and areas of concern. Providing the source of data or information increases validity and provides a basis for program change. Establishing timelines, team roles, and responsibilities will aid in completion of tasks. Finally, assessment criteria help with accountability, and a list of resources that includes time, hardware, software, profession development, etc., should also be included. It is recommended the data team post the data planning matrix online, in the teachers' lounge, and in other workrooms throughout the building.

Cycle of Improvement

The data feedback model is a continuous cycle in which student learning and school improvement are ongoing activities. A systematic approach to data-informed decision-making is required for the system to be successful. Schools without a vertically and horizontally articulated curriculum will find data analysis has limited value. Only when all teachers are communicating with one another about student learning, and becoming immersed in the inquiry process, will data become a tool to increase student achievement. The model provides a workable framework to begin the process.

Best Practices in Data-Informed Decision-Making: A Vignette

"Erika's Story: Test Scores Are More Than Numbers"1

The principal sat at her desk peering over the mountain of numbers. Erika commented that numbers by themselves mean very little. She stated that "you need to get information out of the data" and to ask questions about how data are aligned with school practices. She concluded that standardized test results are important but represent only one type of data. For example, you must drill deeper, asking questions such as: Is English the child's first language? Are there books at home? Are parents engaged in the learning process, helping with homework, and providing students with support?

Erika realized that she needs to understand what takes place in each classroom. Daily walkthroughs provide a glimpse of what happens in the classrooms and also help to set expectations for teachers. She acknowledged trepidation among teachers and administrators because many teachers fear the data will be used against them. Changing the culture was an important part of the process. Erika used the data to begin many conversations focusing on what the teachers could do to increase student learning? The process did not involve finger pointing but rather gaining an understanding of the factors that contributed to low test scores. Erika and her teachers examined student trends, looking at student achievement in previous years. In situations where gaps existed, what were the reasons? Teachers began to understand they could no longer function under the assumption that students begin the new school year with a blank slate. Teachers must know who they have in the classroom and have sufficient information about these students, and any other data that might provide a glimpse into the learning process.

To facilitate this process, a number of structural changes were made. First, a data warehouse was created. The warehouse allowed Erika to present teachers with information on each student at the beginning of the school year. Teachers reviewed data on Grade Level Content Expectations (GLCESs) which are provided by the state and focused on what students need to learn. In addition, during the first month of school, students who needed extra help and support were identified. A team consisting of the principal, teachers, and Title I coordinator was formed to review data and the information was shared with parents. This was not a single meeting but part of a process to provide support to the student and their parents.

Second, communication channels with central office were established. Teachers developed "school improvement readouts" and actually met with central office staff to review building progress. The process involved reviewing building goals and exchanging perspectives on student learning. Conversations provided teachers the opportunity to identify areas that needed additional support and professional development.

Third, school officials established multi-aged classrooms. To strength instruction, math, science, and language arts were departmentalized. Title I funds were used to rehire retired teachers who could provide students additional support. Online remedial programs were purchased to provide students with additional assistance. Time to analyze data was a problem, and the school day was reorganized so that teachers had time to work together to analyze data and develop strategies to address student learning. Each week teachers were provided a half day to focus on curriculum and instruction with data guiding the conversations. Data became part of the school culture as conversations were ongoing. Procedures were enacted where teachers worked in teams to complete reports.

Finally, principal visibility was also important. Being visible in the halls and classrooms, keeping an open door to discuss challenges, and recognizing teachers for outstanding lessons and performance became the norm. Successes needed to be recognized and celebrated. Erika recognized that all the data in the world won't make a difference if teachers were not motivated to use the data.

The school was 99% African American with most families below the poverty line. These systemic efforts resulted in increased student learning. More than 90% of sixth-graders were proficient in reading, language arts, and math; 80% in writing; and 86% social studies. More than 80% of the third, fourth, and fifth graders were proficient in reading, language arts, and math. Math scores increased from the previous year for fifth grade but decreased slightly for third and fourth grade. The trend in language arts also was mixed, showing a strong increase in sixth grade and declines in third, fourth, and fifth grades. Performance was celebrated. Data-informed schools make a difference.

Other Best Practices in Data-Informed Decision-Making

Schools and districts have become part of the accountability movement. One way to promote school awareness is to have data teams annually report student progress to the board of school trustees and to community members. Scheduling sessions at the conclusion of the school year for teachers and administrators to share student progress helps to facilitate data team efforts. Presenting the building profile to the board also allows teachers to showcase accomplishments.

Action plans connected to standardized and formative assessment provide building blocks for improvement. In this activity, content area teachers meet to review strengths and areas where improvement is needed. Once areas are reviewed and questions formulated, teachers make curricular and instructional adjustments. To enhance this process, targets are established for the upcoming school year along with predetermined criteria to determine success. Emphasis is placed on why students are learning or not learning. Grade level-teachers in the preceding grades and teachers in succeeding grades must discuss student achievement. The time-consuming process is something most learning professions must complete if improvements are to occur.

An annual report is another way to showcase accomplishments. In this report, the four types of data are used in a document that highlights the accomplishments of the previous school year and sets targets for the next year. The annual report is disseminated to business and industrial leaders and parents.

Students must also become part of the data review and analysis process. Student-led conferences are a sound framework for engaging students and teachers into the data improvement process. Teachers and students review student achievement on classwork, homework, test, quizzes, reports, and participation. In addition, student attendance and tardiness are reviewed. Students complete profiles of their accomplishments and, in graphs and charts and in a discussion, they present them to the teacher and parents. Student-led conferences give students the opportunity to participate in the accountability process and to take responsibility for their own learning. Teachers also become more data driven as they help students to prepare for conferences. Beginning student-led conferences in the elementary grades will help establish a culture of shared responsibility between teachers and students.

The "best practice" is to create a culture of data use involving all stakeholders. This is easier to accomplish when data are used in multiple ways—such as in board presentations, published action plans aligned with school improvement, and student conferences—to drive the inquiry process. Data-informed decision-making must become routine, and the preferred method to accomplish this is to inculcate data in as many different activities as possible. Using data moves teachers and principals away from intuition and past practice and creates a professional learning community that involves teachers, principals, students, and parents. Above all, data represent a tool to re-engineer and improve education. In no other productive organization, could working processionals cling to previous practices and survive in a competitive marketplace. Education is now at the crossroads. Teachers and administrators must become knowledge workers in the truest sense, make ongoing adjustments, and develop strategies that translate into substantive change and increased student learning.

Resources for Data-Informed Decision-Making

Tools as Resources

Data Dashboard for National Comparisons of Student Progress. The United States Department of Education has developed a data dashboard that provides comparative information related to student learning using multiple measures. The dashboard allows districts to compare student progress in a number of categories. Although data are time sensitive, the website provides an example of how to organize data. The format may be replicated by district officials. http://dashboard.ed.gov

Data-Informed Decision-Making: A Guidebook for Data Points and Analyses in the Context of Michigan School Improvement Framework. This instrument suggests data points and data analysis methods for 26 dimensions of school improvement such as "curriculum alignment, reviewed and monitored" and "curriculum communicated." Please see http://www.wmich.edu/wallacegrant/docs/DIDM.pd for Shen, J., Cooley, V. E., Marx, G., Kirby, E., & Whale, D. E. (2012). Data-Informed Decision-Making: A Guidebook for Data Points and Analyses for the School Improvement Team. In J. Shen (Ed.), *Tools for improving school principals' work* (pp. 137–168). New York: Peter Lang.

Data-Informed Decision-Making on High Impact Strategies: A Measurement Tool for School Principals. This instrument measures principals' level of data-informed decision-making along the 11 high-impact strategies identified by Marzano (2003) as associated with student achievement. Please see Shen, Cooley, Reeves, Burt, Rainey, & Yuan (2012) or http://www.wmich.edu/wallacegrant/docs-/DIDM-INST.pdf

Data for Student Success (D4SS). Michigan Department of Education provides the D4SS tool at no cost to Michigan schools. The on-line tool is used to further the culture of data-driven decision-making in Michigan's schools by providing a quality professional development model and online inquiry tool to analyze student achievement and school process data. Please visithttp://data4ss.org/. Other states and organizations have similar tools for data-informed decision-making.

Annotated Bibliographies for Suggested Readings

Bernhardt, V. L. (2010). *Data, data everywhere: Bringing all the data together for continuous school improvement.* Larchmont, NY: Eye on Education. The book introduces the concepts of data disaggregation and data intersection and connects data analysis to continuous school improvement process.

Boudett, K. P., City, E. A., & Murnane, R. (2006). *Data wise: A step-by-step guide to using assessment results to improve teaching and learning.* Cambridge, MA: Harvard Education Press. The book demonstrates how inquiries into achievement data and other classroom data facilitate school improvement.

Rose, A., Peery, A., Pitchford, B., Doubek, B., Kamm, C., Allison, E., Cordova, J., Nielsen, K., Besser, L., Campsen, L., Gregg, L., White, M., & Ventura, S. (2010). *Data teams: The big picture—looking at data teams through a collaborative lens.* Englewood, CO: Lead and Learn Press. An anthology by practicing experts discusses what data teams are and how the data teams impact educational change at the ground level.

Endnote

1 This vignette was adapted from Colvin, R. L. (n.d.). *Mining for meaning in Michigan's data book: One principal's quest to make numbers count.* Seattle, WA: Center for the Study of Teaching and Policy. Downloadable from http://www.wallacefoundation.org/knowledge-center/school-leadership/effective-principal-leadership/Documents/Mining-for-Meaning-in-Michigan-Data-Book.pdf

References

Bernhardt, V. (1998). *Data analysis for comprehensive schoolwide improvement.* Larchmont, NY: Eye on Education.

Bernhardt, V. (2004). *Data analysis for continuous school improvement* (2nd ed.). Larchmont, NY: Eye on Education.

Bernhardt, V. L. (2010). *Data, data everywhere: Bringing all the data together for continuous school improvement.* Larchmont, NY: Eye on Education.

Black, P., & Wiliam, D. (1998). Inside the black box. *Phi Delta Kappan, 80*(2), 139–148.

Bolman, L. G., & Deal, T .E. (2003). *Reframing organizations: Artistry, choice and leadership* (3rd ed.)San Francisco, CA: Jossey-Bass.

Borman, G. D. (2002). Reinventing education. *Peabody Journal of Education, 77*(4), 7–27.

Boudett, K. P., City, E. A., & Murnane, R. (2006). *Data wise: A step-by-step guide to using assessment results to improve teaching and learning.* Cambridge, MA: Harvard Education Press.

Bounds, G., Dobbins, G., & Fowler, O. (1995). *Management: A total quality perspective.* Cincinnati, OH: South-Western College Publishing.

Brown, R., & Lemke, C. (2007). *Informed decision making and higher student achievement.* Retrieved from www.metiri.com/PDFs/MetiriSDP.pdf.

Choppin, J. (2002). *Data use in practice: Examples from the school level.* Paper presented at the annual meeting of the American Educational Research Association, New Orleans, LA.

Chrispeels, J. H., Brown, J. H., & Castillo, S. (2000). School leadership teams: Factors that influence their development and effectiveness. *Advances in Research and Theories of School Management and Educational Policy, 4,* 39–73.

Chubb, J. E., & Moe, T. M. (1990). *Politics, markets, and America's schools.* Washington, DC: The Brookings Institute.

Cook, T. D. (2001). Science phobia: Why education researchers reject randomized experiments. *Education Next, 1*(3), 63–68.

Dahlkemper, L. (2002). School board leadership: Using data for school improvement. *NSBA Policy Research Brief, 27*(1), 1–4

Earl, L., & Katz, S. (2006). *Leading schools in a data-rich world: Harnessing data for school improvement.* Thousand Oaks, CA: Corwin.

Edmonds, R. (1979). Effective schools for the urban poor. *Educational Leadership, 37*(1), 15–27.

Ericsson, F. (2007). Some thoughts on "proximal" formative assessment of student learning. *Yearbook for the National Society for the Study of Education, 106*(1), 186–216.

Feldman, J., & Tung, R. (2001). Using data-based inquiry and decision making to improve instruction. *ERS Spectrum 19*(3), 10–19.

Grayson, C. J. Jr. (2006). The proof is in the processes: The missing link in improving K-12 education and meeting NCLB goals in process management. *Teaching & Learning, 26*(11), 28.

Halverson, R. (2010). School formative feedback systems. *Peabody Journal of Education, 85*, 130–146.

Hamilton, L., Halverson, R., Jackson, S., Mandinach, E., Supovitz, J., & Wayman, J. (2009). *Using student achievement data to support instructional decision making* (NCEE 2009–4067). Washington, DC: National Center for Education Evaluation and Regional Assistance, Institute of Education Sciences, U.S. Department of Education.

Haycock, K. (1998). Good teaching matters . . . a lot. *Thinking K-16, 3*(2), 1–14.

Ikemoto, G. S., & Marsh, J. A. (2007). Cutting through the "data-driven" mantra: Different conceptions of data-driven decision making. In P. Moss (Ed.), *Evidence and decision making* (106th *Yearbook of the National Society for the Study of Education*; (pp. 105–131). Malden, MA: Blackwell.

Jackson, S. A., & Lunenburg, F. C. (2010). School performance indicators, accountability ratings, and student achievement. *American Secondary Education, 39*(1), 27–44.

Keeney, L. (1998). *Using data for school improvement: Report on the second practitioner's conference for Annenberg Challenge Sites.* Providence, RI.

Knapp, M. S., Copland, M. A, & Swinnerton, J. A. (2007). Introduction: Evidence and decision-making. In P. Moss (Ed.), *Evidence and decision making* (106th *Yearbook of the National Society for the Study of Education*; (pp. 74–104). Malden, MA: Blackwell.

Koretz, D. (2003). Using multiple measures to address perverse incentives and score inflation. *Educational Measurement: Issues and Practice, 22*(2), 18–26.

Kowalski, T. J., Lasley II, T. J., & Mahoney, J. W. (2008). *Data-driven decision and school leadership: Best practices for school improvement.* Boston, MA: Pearson.

Lachat, M. A., & Smith, S. (2005). Practices that support data use in urban high schools. *Journal of Education for Students Placed at Risk (JESPAR), 10*(3), 333–349.

Marsh, J. A., Payne, J. F., & Hamilton, L. S. (2006). *Making sense of data-driven decision making in education.* Santa Monica, CA: RAND Corporation.

Marzano, R. J. (2003). *What works in schools.* Alexandria, VA: Association of Supervision and Curriculum Development.

Marzano, R. J., Waters, T., & McNulty, B. A. (2005). *School leadership that works: From research to results.* Alexandria, VA: Association of Supervision and Curriculum Development.

Mason, S. (2002). *Turning data into knowledge: Lessons from six Milwaukee public schools.* Madison, WI: Wisconsin Center for Educational Research.

Moss, P. A., & Piety, P. F. (2007). Introduction: Evidence and decision-making. In P. Moss (Ed.), *Evidence and decision making* (106th *Yearbook of the National Society for the Study of Education*; (pp. 1–14). Malden, MA: Blackwell.

Popham, W. J. (2008). *Transformational assessment.* Alexandria, VA: Association for Supervision and Curriculum Development.

Ramaprasad, A. (1983). On the definition of feedback. *Behavioral Science, 28*(1), 4–13.

Reeves, D. B. (2010). *Transforming professional development into student results.* Alexandria, VA: Association for Supervision and Curriculum Development.

Reynolds, D., & Teddlie, C. (2000). *The international handbook of school effectiveness research.* London: Falmer.

Rose, A., Peery, A., Pitchford, B., Doubek, B., Kamm, C., Allison, E., Cordova, J., Nielsen, K., Besser, L., Campsen, L., Gregg, L., White, M., & Ventura, S. (2010). *Data teams: The big picture—looking at data teams through a collaborative lens.* Englewood, CO: Lead and Learn.

Sadler, D. (1989). Formative assessment and the design of instructional systems. *Instructional Science, 18*(2),119–144.

Senge, P. M. (1990). *The fifth discipline: The art and practice of a learning organization.* New York: Doubleday.

Shen, J., & Cooley, V. E. (2008). Critical issues in using data for decision-making. *International Journal of Leadership in Education,11*(3), 319–329.

Shen, J., Cooley, V. E., Marx, G., Kirby, E., & Whale, D. E. (2012). Data-Informed Decision-Making: A Guidebook for Data Points and Analyses for the School Improvement Team. In J. Shen (Ed.), *Tools for improving school principals' work* (pp. 137–168). New York: Peter Lang.

Shen, J., Cooley, V., Ma, X., Reeves, P., Burt, W., Rainey, M., & Yuan, W. (2012). Data-informed decision-making on high impact strategies: Developing and validating a measurement tool for principals. *Journal of Experimental Education, 80*(1), 1–25.

Shen, J., Cooley, V. E., Reeves, P., Burt, W. L., Ryan, L., Rainey, J. M., & Wenhui, Y. (2010). Using data for decision-making: Perspectives from 16 principals in Michigan, USA. *International Review of Education, 56*, 435–456.

Stringfield, S. (1994). Outlier studies of school effects. In D. Reynolds, B. Creemers, P. Nesselrodt et al., *Advances in school effectiveness: Research and practice.* Oxford: Pergamon.

Supovitz, J. A., & Klein, V. (2003). *Mapping a course for improved learning: How innovative schools systematically use student performance data to guide instruction.* Philadelphia, PA: Consortium for Policy Research in Education.

Van Barneveld, C. (2008). Using data to improve student achievement, What works? *Research into Practice series 15.* The Literacy and Numeracy Secretariat and the Ontario Association of Deans of Education. Retrieved from http://www.edu.gov.on.ca/eng/literacynumeracy/inspire/research/Using_Data.pdf

Wayman, J. C. (2005). Involving teachers in data-driven decision making: Using computer data systems to support teacher inquiry and reflection. *Journal of Education for Students Placed at Risk, 10*(3), 295–308.

3

Safe and Orderly School Operations

DENNIS C. McCRUMB AND ROBERT J. LENEWAY

Introduction

Maintaining a safe and orderly environment is critical to the success of any school. Lezotte and McKee (2002) state, "In the effective school, we say there is an orderly, purposeful, business-like atmosphere, which is free from the threat of physical harm. The school climate is not oppressive and is conducive to teaching and learning" (p. 17). Lezotte and McKee stress that safety while at school is the number one priority of parents. Developing and maintaining a safe and orderly school is a complex endeavor requiring leadership, planning, management, supervision, and attention to detail. To become an orderly school, building principals must consider multiple factors including school safety, culture, climate, bullying, discipline and positive student behavior, and safe use of technology.

Safety is a huge issue brought to the national forefront by the catastrophe at Columbine High School in Littleton, Colorado as well as violence and shootings in other schools around the country. Unfortunately, these tragedies have not been only limited to classrooms but all areas of education. In the small town of Chelsea, Michigan a science teacher shot and killed the superintendent and wounded both the building principal and another teacher after an unsatisfactory disciplinary hearing. In 1994, a man walked into Dade County superintendent Dr. James

Adam's office and killed him. Schools across the country are conscious of the threat of violence and have enacted safety programs which include visitor sign-in, badges, metal detectors, locked entry doors and other preventive measures.

"Good schools are characterized by high standards, high expectations, and a caring environment. Good schools are also invariably orderly places" (Ubben, Hughes, & Norris, 2010, p. 86). Standards and expectations must be known and supported by the entire school community (Ubben et al., 2010).

Schools are under tremendous pressure to improve student achievement and are being subjected to regulations and standards defining the level at which students should be achieving. No Child Left Behind (NCLB) prescribes an incremental path for student achievement that all schools must attain or face consequences. These consequences include students leaving to attend other schools, principals being replaced, or districts taken over by the state. Establishing and maintaining a safe and orderly school is closely connected to student learning.

Both school administrators and researchers have discovered a "missing link" in the school improvement problem. This missing link has more to do with a positive school culture than with major curriculum reform, testing programs, and other school reform efforts (Wagner & Hall-O'Phelan, 1998). Other authors (Levine & Lezotte, 1995; Phillips, 1996; Peterson & Deal, 1998; Frieberg, 1998) describe school climate and culture as exceedingly important, but they are often overlooked as an integral part of the school improvement process. If school culture is not positive, collegial and professional, productivity is likely to flounder (Peterson & Deal, 2002). Teachers and students who do not feel safe will not have the necessary psychological energy for teaching and learning, which results in the school having a limited opportunity to improve student achievement (Marzano, 2003).

School culture is one of the components of an orderly school. Other factors in maintaining an orderly school include school climate, personnel management, bullying, safety, and discipline. Unless they address each of these issues, school leaders will encounter daunting challenges in their efforts to increase student achievement.

Connecting individualized learning and high stakes accountability while maintaining orderly school operation in the 21st century, requires a new type of educational leader. A struggle has emerged to meet student, parent, and teacher needs while concurrently addressing increasing demands for accountability by school boards and state and federal government officials. In the past, it was sufficient for principals to be good managers, but the demands of the 21st century require leadership, vigilance, and targeted actionable behavior from building principals.

Research Evidence on the Relationship Between Student Achievement and Safe and Orderly School

There is a growing body of evidence that orderly schools with positive climates promote and enhance student achievement. Lezotte and McKee (2002) refined and expanded Lezotte's work on effective schools. His current concept of effective schools includes the following seven elements:

1. Instructional leadership
2. Clear and focused mission
3. Safe and orderly environment
4. Climate of high expectations
5. Frequent monitoring of student progress
6. Positive home-school relations
7. Opportunity to learn and time on task

Lezotte and McKee emphasize effective schools are characterized by "an orderly, purposeful, business-like atmosphere, which is free from the threat of physical harm. The school climate is not oppressive and is conducive to teaching and learning" (p. 17).

Marzano (2001, p. 56) researched effective practices in schools that increase student achievement. He identified three levels of factors that lead to improved student learning. School, teacher, and student level factors all play a role. Table 3.1 ranks the school-level factors related to high student achievement.

Table 3.1 Marzano's School-Level Factors by Rank

Rank	Factor
1	Opportunity to Learn
2	Time
3	Monitoring
4	Pressure to Achieve
5	Parental Involvement
6	School Climate
7	Leadership
8	Cooperation

Adapted by permission of McREL (Mid-continent Research for Education and Learning) (Organization) & Educational Resources Information Center (U.S.). Marzano, R. J. (2001). *A new era of school reform: Going where the research takes us.* Aurora, CO: Mid-continent Research for Education and Learning.

Marzano identified climate as one of the school factors related to increased student achievement. His findings support the work of Lezotte and other researchers. Marzano (2003) compared the research on school-level factors in reference to increased student learning and ranked these factors by impact on student achievement. Table 3.2 provides a synthesis of school-level factors from multiple researchers. All five researchers concurred that a requirement for improved student achievement is a safe and orderly environment.

Table 3.2 Comparison of School-Level Factors

Comparing School-Level Factors Across Researchers						
School-level Factors	Rank	Marzano	Scheerens and Bosker	Sammons	Levine and Lezotte	Edmonds
Guaranteed and Viable Curriculum	1	Opportunity to Learn, Time	Content Coverage, Time	Concentration on Teaching and Learning	Focus on Central Learning Skills	Emphasis on Basic Skill Acquisition
Challenging Goals and Effective Feedback	2	Monitoring Pressure to Achieve	Monitoring Pressure to Achieve	High Expectations Monitoring Progress	High Expectations and Requirements, Monitoring	High Expectations for Student Success, Frequent Monitoring
Parental and Community Involvement	3	Parental Involvement	Parental Involvement	Home–School Partnership	Salient Parental Involvement	
Safe and Orderly Environment	4	*School Climate*	*School Climate*	*Learning Environment, Positive Reinforcement, Pupil Rights and Expectations*	*Productive Climate and Culture*	*Safe and Orderly Atmosphere Conducive to Learning*
Collegiality and Professionalism	5	Leadership Cooperation	Leadership Cooperation	Professional Leadership, Shared Vision and Goals, Learning Organization	Strong Leadership, Practice-Oriented Staff Development	Strong Administrative Leadership

From Robert J. Marzano, *What works in schools: Translating research into action* (p. 19), Alexandria, VA: ASCD. © 2003 by ASCD. Reprinted with permission. Learn more about ASCD at www.ascd.org

Key Concepts in Safe and Orderly School Operations

Culture

School cultures range from positive to toxic and yield considerable influence over the way people think, act, and behave. Barth (2002) observed "A school's culture is a complex pattern of norms, attitudes, beliefs, behaviors, values, ceremonies, traditions, and myths that are deeply ingrained in the very core of the organization"

(p. 6). Deal and Peterson (2009) defined culture as the "underlining set of norms, values, beliefs, rituals, and traditions that make up the unwritten rules of how to think, feel, and act in an organization" (p. 108). Robbins (2002) described culture as "an inner reality that influences the way people interact, what they will and will not do, and what they value as 'right and rude'" (p. 42). Culture includes common norms, values, rituals, and beliefs that determine individual and organizational behavior.

Cultures are the most important (and perhaps the most misunderstood element of a school) and the most difficult to change (Barth, 2002). If the school culture is negative, the principal must identify the causes to determine the issues triggering the negativity. Barth (2002) describes "nondiscussables" as subjects important enough to be discussed in open settings but on which public discussions create fear and anxiety. As a result, these conversations usually take place in parking lots, restrooms, play grounds, car pools, or the dinner table at home. "The health of a school is inversely proportional to the number of nondiscussables: the fewer nondiscussables, the healthier the school; the more nondiscussables, the more pathology in the school culture" (Barth, 2002, p. 7). When the school environment remains toxic, student achievement suffers if the principal does not openly address issues and seek solutions. The number of at-risk students tends to increase when the school culture remains unhealthy.

Principals must understand and be able to implement the elements of a positive school culture. Deal and Peterson (2009) list five components of such a culture.

1. A shared sense of purpose and values among staff.
2. Group norms of continuous learning, and the group reinforces the importance of staff learning with a focus on school improvement.
3. A sense of responsibility for student learning shared by all staff.
4. Collaborative and collegial relationships between staff members.
5. A focus on professional development, staff reflection, and sharing of professional practice.

Four elements support school improvement—improvement of teachers' skills, the systematic review and adaptation of curriculum, improvement of the organization, and the participation of parents in an organized school–community partnership. Underlying these four strands is a culture that will either positively influence or undermine these interrelated elements (Saphier & King, 1985).

Saphier and King (1985) identified 12 cultural norms that assist principals in improving schools by changing the culture.

1. Collegiality
2. Experimentation
3. High expectations
4. Trust and confidence
5. Tangible support
6. Reaching out to the knowledge base
7. Appreciation and recognition
8. Caring, celebration, and humor
9. Involvement in decision making
10. Protection of what's important
11. Traditions
12. Honest, open communication

Principals who support and implement these norms increase the probability that their school will have a positive school culture which will translate into school improvement. Principals shape the culture of their school on a daily basis by their interactions with staff, students, community, and parents (Peterson, n.d.).

According to Tableman and Herron, in the *Best Practice Briefs* (2004) compiled at Michigan State University, a positive culture is developed over time. The *Best Practice Briefs* (2004) suggest several practices to help maintain a positive culture (p. 2).

Practices that Support Learning:

Artifacts and symbols–Arrangements in the building reflect the children, their needs, and their accomplishments.

Values–All school stakeholders participate in decision making.

Assumptions and beliefs–Teachers and parents believe all students can learn and parents want their children to be successful.

Practices that Impede Learning:

Artifacts and symbols–Very little in the building demonstrates an emphasis on children and what they are learning.

Values–Decisions are made without stakeholder input (teachers and parents).

Assumptions and beliefs–Education is not important to parents and teachers and parents believe that some students are not capable or too lazy to learn.

The information above lists practices that support and those that impede the learning process. These actions are critical to the well-being of students, parents, teachers, and administrators, and the overall vitality of the learning process.

Changing Culture

After a school's culture has been analyzed and understood, it is the responsibility of the principal to lead the charge for change. Principals can assist in building a positive culture by taking the following steps (Deal & Peterson, 2009):

1. Reinforce positive elements of the school's culture.
2. Transform the negative elements.
3. Keep all interaction positive, because every interaction helps shape the culture.

The Center for Improving School Culture also suggests practices that help to maintain a positive culture:

1. Develop common beliefs, visions, and values that are communicated and enforced.
2. Identify heroes and heroines whose actions and accomplishments embody these values.
3. Celebrate rituals and ceremonies that reinforce these values.
4. Develop stories that reflect the goals and standards of the organization.

Derpak and Yarema (2002) indicated that by maintaining a few proven core values leaders can develop a positive culture. They suggested three such core values along with action items that support a positive school climate.

1. Be thoughtful and make people feel special
    a. First impressions are important
    b. People like to be thanked
    c. A meet and greet program shows hospitality
    d. Illustrate school life with a hallway photo board
    e. Celebrate birthdays
    f. Create fun activities for students

2. Get people involved
    a. Take an idea and turn it into an event
    b. Get parents involved
    c. Solicit student suggestions and take them seriously

3. Recognize and reward positive behavior
    a. Make report cards look extra special
    b. Recognize positive actions of staff and students

Climate

Perry was the first educator to observe and write about the way that a school's climate affects student learning (Perry, 1908). Studying school climate systematically evolved from contemporary organizational research and studies on school effectiveness (Creemers & Reezigt, 1999; Kreft, 1993; Miller & Fredericks, 1990).

Numerous studies support the positive impact of school climate on student performance and the well-being of students, teachers, and the school environment. Two elements of school climate include a commitment to school and positive feedback from teachers. These elements positively impact student self-esteem, which, in turn, affects student learning (Hoge et al., 1990). Research has also pointed out negative relationships between school climate and absenteeism (DeJung & Duckworth, 1986; Rumberger, 1987; Sommer, 1985) and the rate of suspensions from school (Wu, Pink, Crain, & Moles, 1982). A positive and sustained school climate enhances and promotes student academic achievement (Cohen, Pickeral, & McCloskey, 2009).

A school's climate is the compilation of the totality of interactions by all people, both positive and negative, that take place each day (Goleman, 2006). Staff unconsciously promote school climate even though they may not be aware their daily activities are contributing to school climate. It is obvious that messages may be mixed with no guarantee that positive messages are being shared. This presents a challenge to the building leadership and stakeholders. Teachers, administrators, and support staff are obligated to perform their duties and interact positively to support a productive school climate.

Principals carry the heaviest burden in setting the tone for a positive climate. Goleman, Boyatzis, and McKee (2004) identified six leadership styles and discussed how each affects school climate. These styles are:

Visionary—articulates shared goals and provides feedback on the goals.

Coaching—works individually with people and provides feedback and suggestions on their assignments.

Democratic—listens and asks for input at the appropriate time, draws on the knowledge of others.

Affiliative—builds emotional capital, having fun is good for the organization.
Pacesetting—leads by example with high expectations.
Commanding—give orders and demands immediate responses, coercive.

The visionary, coaching, democratic, and affiliative styles promote a positive climate that helps to create an atmosphere in which teachers and students want to do their best. Pacesetting and commanding leadership styles often contribute to negative climates that inhibit positive working relationships and student performance (Goleman, Boyatzis, & McKee, 2004). A study by the Hay Group (2000) in Great Britain found teachers were most productive and satisfied when they perceived the principal acted as follows:

1. Led with flexibility rather than always abiding by the rules.
2. Let teachers use their own teaching methods, but held them accountable for results.
3. Set realistic goals that were challenging and appropriate.
4. Valued the teachers' work and provided recognition when they excelled.

Principal leadership is crucial to a healthy climate, which is closely related to a school's culture. "The feelings and attitudes that are elicited by a schools' environment are referred to as school climate" (Loukas, 2007, p. 1). Loukas divided that school climate into three dimensions as illustrated in Table 3.3.

Table 3.3 School Climate Dimensions

Physical Dimension	Social Dimension	Academic Dimension
Appearance of the school building and its classrooms	Quality of interpersonal relationships between and among students, teachers, and staff	Quality of instruction
School size and ratio of students to teachers in the classroom	Equitable and fair treatment of students by teachers and staff	Teacher expectations for student achievement
Order and organization of classrooms in the school	Degree of competition and social comparison between students	Monitoring student progress and promptly reporting results to students and parents
Availability of resources	Degree to which students, teachers, and staff contribute to decision-making at the school	
Safety and comfort		

These three interrelated dimensions must be implemented in a systematic fashion to develop a productive teaching and learning environment. "School climate reflects the physical and psychological aspects of the school that are more susceptible to change and that provide the preconditions necessary for teaching and learning to take place" (Tableman & Herron, 2004, p. 2). Tableman and Herron (2004) reviewed the research and summarized the findings related to school climate. Tableman and Herron identified four environmental factors and with actions that support and impede learning.

Factors That Support Learning:

Physical Environment–

- Enrollment is limited
- Students feel safe
- Orderly classrooms
- Building is clean and grounds are maintained
- Appropriate noise levels
- Appropriate instructional areas
- Sufficient textbooks and supplies exist

Social Environment–

- Principal encourages interaction between teachers and students
- Students and staff participate in decision making
- Training is provided for staff and students for preventing and resolving conflict

Affective Environment–

- Interactions are caring, responsive, supportive, and respectful
- Trust exists between students and staff
- Morale is high
- Staff and students are friendly
- The school embraces diversity
- Teachers, staff, and students are respected and valued
- There is a sense of community
- Parents perceive the school as warm, caring, and inviting

Academic Environment–

- There is an emphasis on academics and all learning styles are embraced
- High expectations for all
- Progress is monitored regularly
- Assessment results are promptly communicated
- Achievements and performance are rewarded and praised
- Teachers are knowledgeable and confident

Factors That Impede Learning:

Physical Environment–

- Large student enrollment
- Students harass each other
- Classrooms are disorganized
- School is unclean and grounds not maintained
- Noisy environment
- Classes in rooms not intended for that use
- Insufficient textbooks and supplies

Social Environment–

- Limited interaction between teachers and students
- Central office and the principal make all decisions
- Students are not part of the decision-making process
- Bullying and conflicts are ignored

Affective Environment–

- Limited interaction between teachers and students
- Students perceive teachers and staff as not acting in their best interest
- Morale is low among teachers and staff
- Staff and students are not friendly
- Diversity is not embraced
- Teachers feel unappreciated and there is little positive reinforcement for students
- There is no feeling of community within the school
- Parents feel unwelcome at the school

Academic Environment–

- Academic performance is not rewarded
- Low expectations exist
- Assessment results are not communicated in a timely manner or at all
- Assessment data are not used to improve instruction
- Minimal rewards and praise
- Teachers are not properly prepared

The National School Climate Council (2012) (http://www.schoolclimate.org) suggests four major categories that promote a positive school climate. These include (1) safety, (2) teaching and learning, (3) relationships, and (4) the institutional environment.

Developing a positive school climate does not occur by happenstance. Leaders must take systematic steps to develop and nurture such a climate. Ubben, Hughes, and Norris (2010) have nine suggestions for developing a positive school climate:

1. Celebrate the positive.
2. Create rituals and ceremonies.
3. Shield and support the possible.
4. Confront and eradicate the negative influences.
5. Provide consistency.
6. Provide role models.
7. Focus on recruitment and retention of quality staff.
8. Clean up and clear out.
9. Create and share the new stories of success and accomplishment.

Bullying

Bullying will prevent the formation of a positive climate: it has become epidemic with legal and sociological ramifications that severely compromise the teaching and learning environment. Olweus (1993, p. 1) defines bullying in the following manner: "A person is bullied when he or she is exposed, repeatedly and over time, to negative actions on the part of one or more other persons, and he or she has difficulty defending himself or herself." Bullying can take many forms—verbal, social exclusion, physical, threats, racial, sexual, and cyberbullying (Olweus, 1993). Sophisticated analyses of data collected from thousands of students in Canada seem to indicate that there is a reciprocal relationship between bullies and victims. In other words, bullies themselves are victims (Ma, 2001).

Bullying and a Protected Class

Many teachers and administrators fail to recognize that bullying is a violation of state and federal law. Recent bullying cases leading to student suicide have raised the national consciousness as to the scope and severity of bullying. Student bullying that causes discrimination against any protected class and creates a hostile environment is a violation of law with sanctions for the bully and school officials should they fail to act in a responsible fashion. Bullying may result in a violation of a student's civil rights if it is "sufficiently severe, pervasive, and persistent" (Hutton & Bailey, 2007) that it negatively interferes with a student's ability to participate in and enjoy the benefits of school. Bullied students tend to do poorly in school. Their grades suffer, they are prone to depression, have low self-esteem, and may develop health problems (Olweus, 1993). School districts receiving federal funding through the Department of Education share a legal obligation to abide by these federal laws, which means enforcing anti-discrimination policies as they apply to instances of discriminatory bullying to protect the civil rights of all students. Schools can be held liable for the failure of their teachers to prevent bullying on the basis of discrimination against a protected class.

The North Carolina Department of Juvenile Justice and Delinquency Prevention Center for the Prevention of School Violence compiled the following statistics on bullying:

- 77% of students are bullied in some manner.
- 8% of students miss 1 day of class per month for fear of bullies.
- 43% fear harassment in the bathroom at school.
- 100,000 students carry guns to school every year.
- 28% of students who carry weapons have witnessed violence at home.
- 1 out of 5 students admits to being a bully.
- Playground statistics show that every 7 minutes a child is bullied.

Schools having lower rates of bullying and violence tend to have the following characteristics (Johnson, 2009):

1. Students have positive relationships with teachers.
2. Students are aware of school rules and believe they are fair.

3. Students have ownership in their school.
4. Classroom and school environments are positive and focused on student learning.
5. School safety interventions are focused on improving the physical environment of the school.

Cyberbullying

The emergence of new technologies in the schools along with easier internet access calls for the creation of acceptable use policies that include provision for safe internet surfing and the reorganization and control of cyberbullying. The U.S. Department of Justice has developed a model policy for schools to customize according to their needs (http://www.justice.gov/criminal/cybercrime/rules/acceptableUsePolicy.htm). It is important to note that any policy should be discussed and signed by students and/or parents at the start of the school year. Such policies need to clearly communicate the consequences for violations of privacy rights, security of electronic devices, protection of intellectual property, and otherwise "electronically respect and practice the principles of community" (Cybercrime.gov, 2010; http://www.justice.gov/criminal/cybercrime/rules/acceptableUsePolicy.htm).

In a 2008 study, Leneway and Winters found cyberbullying has been largely overlooked by school leadership although it was widely practiced among the students studied. A sample of 58 eighth graders revealed that approximately 29% had been victims of cyberbullying and, incredibly, 24% had bullied someone online. In fact, of those who had admitted to being cyberbullied, 59% admitted to bullying someone else. In addition, approximately 80% of the students reported that they are aware of instances of cyberbullying although the school administrators reported that they knew of no incidents.

Olweus (1993) suggests three interrelated reasons why bullying takes place.

1. These students have a strong need for power and negative dominance.
2. Students find satisfaction in causing injury and/or suffering to others.
3. Students who bully often receive material or psychological rewards for their behavior.

Olweus also describes the concept of a "bullying circle." This includes students who in some manner surround and form a circle around the student being bullied.

1. Students who bully—play a lead role in bullying
2. Followers or henchmen—do not initiate bullying but take an active role
3. Supporters or passive bullies—support and watch bullying but don't join in
4. Passive supporters or possible bullies—like bullying but do not show outward signs of support
5. Disengaged onlookers—do not get involved or take a stand
6. Possible defenders—do not like bullying and think they should help those being bullied
7. Defenders—do not like bullying and try to help those being bullied

Courts have been very clear on this issue, and schools should develop policies to outline best practices in handling students who bully.

Discipline and Positive Student Control

Numerous studies report steps that can be taken to maximize productive school environment and student control (e.g., Ubben, Hughes, & Norris, 2010). These steps include:

1. Clear, firm, and high teacher and administrator expectations
2. Consistent rules and consequences that directly relate to breaking these rules
3. A program emphasizing self-esteem of all students
4. Acknowledging and rewarding positive behavior by students

Studies suggest discipline issues occur when students are not involved in extracurricular activities or are not bonding with the other students (Rauhauser & McLennan, 1995).

Glasser (1986) states in his work on Reality Therapy and Control Theory that students need consequences for their behavior but should also be asked the following four questions when they misbehave.

1. What are you doing?
2. What do you want?
3. Did you get what you wanted?
4. What can you do differently next time to get what you want?

Reality Therapy has been used for decades and is still applicable as students must become part of the remediation process.

Positive Behavior Support (PBS) is a program that is gaining legitimacy in many schools. The goal of PBS is to provide students positive direction and to minimize or eliminate negative behavior issues. Positive Behavior Support offers specific rules and consequences with recognition for positive behavior. Fox and Duda (n.d.) offer six steps that they suggest are critical to a successful Positive Behavior Support program:

1. Build a behavior support team.
2. Planning must be person centered.
3. Have a functional behavioral assessment.
4. Develop a hypothesis.
5. Develop a behavior support plan.
6. Monitor the outcomes and support the plan.

Collaborative Problem Solving (Greene, 2011) teaches adults different ways of understanding student behavior, communicating with misbehaving students, and working with students to solve the problem that initiated that behavior. Greene theorizes that students who misbehave have "lagging skills" that cause the behavior issues. Collaborative Problem Solving is conceptually built around six themes:

1. Kids do well if they can.
2. Doing well is preferable to not doing well.
3. Challenging behavior must be viewed in the context of a child's development.
4. Behind every challenging behavior is a lagging skill and a demand for that skill.
5. Problems should be solved proactively rather than emergently.
6. Problems should be solved collaboratively rather than unilaterally.

Discipline is a complex phenomenon and requires an understanding of curriculum, instruction, child development, and the reasons for student misbehavior. Many teachers are ill equipped to address the problems students bring to school, and, as a result, a cycle of ineffectiveness occurs.

Safe Schools

Violence in schools is an unfortunate reality in today's society. Statistics reveal that 63 out of every 1,000 students in this country are victims of some type of violence at school (Johnson, 2009). These victims of violence at school are more likely to have feelings of isolation, depression, frustration, and less school attachment. These students are also more likely to skip school because of the fear of violence (Johnson, 2009). Threats of violence become a major concern for students.

Marzano (2003) noted the profound negative impact of violence and disorder in schools. He found "students in schools with a high level of violence had lower math scores by 0.20 of a standard deviation and were 5.7 percentage points less likely to graduate" (p. 54). According to Marzano, "A strong relationship exists between truancy and criminal activity" (p. 54). Schools that do not treat a safe and orderly environment as a critical factor in school success undermine other school improvement efforts (Marzano, 2003).

A review of 25 school violence studies (Johnson, 2009) revealed that lower rates of school violence were associated with the following conditions:

1. Positive teacher relationships
2. Students having feelings of ownership of their school
3. Positive environments in the school and classroom that are positive and focus on student comprehension
4. Safety procedures that focus on improving the physical environment and reducing physical disorder

Walker et al. (1995) believe safe schools are characterized by a combination of support mechanisms, teacher and administrator actions, and rules and regulations that include the following:

1. Designate personnel to support students, staff and parents.
2. Offer instruction to all students concerning self-awareness, social relationships and skills, and personal development.
3. Create and maintain a perception of belonging to the school.
4. Recognize students when they succeed in any endeavor.
5. Employ principals who are strong leaders and create a positive environment.
6. Develop principals to be transformational leaders.
7. Encourage cohesiveness among teachers and administrators.
8. Stress classroom environments that emphasize cooperation.

9. Promote shared decision making by staff and students.
10. Ensure rules are enforced and fairly administered.
11. Promote parent involvement in the school.

Although the list seems exhaustive at first glance, teachers and administrators are advised to pay close attention to this research and to develop procedures to address student problems.

Establishing a Shared Vision

Developing a shared vision in conjunction with an overall perspective on a school's goals is crucial in establishing and maintaining orderly school operation. Sociologist Philip Selznick (1957) claims the most important role of a leader is to clearly identify and articulate the vision of the organization. It can be argued that most important characteristics of leaders are commitment and integrity (Searcy, Hall & Edwards, 2000). Too many administrators are devoid of the vision needed to move beyond daily operations and crises. Administrators often strive to be seen as leaders, thus they are continually looking for a parade to get in front of while looking over their shoulder to make sure the parade is still going in their direction. Although the vision of the district should already be established by the superintendent, school boards, and the community, local schools also need a clear understanding and statement of the larger district goals and vision that will be translated into daily orderly operations. Inspired school leadership and orderly school operations begin by establishing a shared vision, developed and embraced by everyone in the school. This activity begins with a discussion on the purpose of the school. An honest and open ongoing discussion can go a long way to developing a shared vision. "Principals should also reflect on their motivations; hire supportive staff; introduce community members; acquaint staff with community needs, characteristics, and key individuals; converse with community groups; select a representative review committee; and publicize the vision" (Krajewski & Matkin, 1996).

Subordinates will not support the vision unless they trust the leader. Many leaders believe that a good cause justifies support, but that is not necessarily the case—subordinates buy into the leader first and then the cause (Maxwell, 1998). "Every message that people receive is filtered through the messenger who delivers it. If you consider the messenger to be credible, then you believe the message has value" (p. 146).

The Role of Technology in a Safe and Orderly Environment

Technology is a tool principals can use to provide a safe and orderly environment. Becoming a manager with the technology tools to support the management role is critical to the principal's success. In the business world, technology has been effectively employed to reduce the demands of routine management tasks and prepare for possible crises, but school management for the most part has lagged behind in the use of informational technology to promote safe and orderly school operations.

Robbins (2002, p. 12) indicates that a manager acts as the brain of a school. Managers establish a system of rules and regulations and even create incentive programs. Effective management strategies are needed for establishing and maintaining safe and orderly environments that can move organizations forward to greater levels of achievement. Technology can be leveraged to improve the operation, safety, and maintenance of 21st-century schools. For example, school management software (SMS) can assist with routine issues such as student scheduling, attendance reporting, grade reporting, discipline monitoring, fee accounting, and health monitoring. This technology can also help with student enrollment, advance planning of teacher assignments, class assignments, student time-tables, bus routes, attendance tracking and a centralized school calendar. Management software can print mailing labels, manage emergency information, keep track of parent volunteers, and display student photos. Technologically savvy leaders use powerful data mining tools to evaluate operations and prepare reports. However, technology is only a tool, and it is what leaders do with the data that may impact how students behave and influence the school climate and culture.

Leaders must continue to use technology to support management and leadership functions. A number of promising technologies enhance school safety while saving time for leaders to work more closely with students, teachers, and parents.

Best Practice

Marzano (2003, pp. 55–58) suggests five action steps to achieve a safe and orderly environment.

1. Establish rules and procedures for behavioral problems that might be caused by the school's physical characteristics or routine.
   - Reduce crowd density by using all entrances and exits to a given area.
   - Keep wait time to enter and exit common areas to a minimum.
   - Decrease travel time and distances between activities and events.

- Use signs marking transitions from less- controlled to more-controlled space.
- Use signs indicating behavioral expectations in common areas.
- Sequence events in common areas to decrease the potential of overcrowding.

2. Establish clear school-wide rules and procedures for general misbehavior, which could include but is not limited to:
   - Bullying
   - Verbal harassment
   - Drug use
   - Obscene language and gestures
   - Gang behavior
   - Sexual harassment
   - Repeated class disruptions
   - Disregarding others' safety and privacy
   - Fighting
   - Theft
   - Truancy
3. Establish and enforce appropriate consequences for violations of rules and procedures.
4. Establish a program that teaches self-discipline and responsibility to students.
5. Establish a system that allows for the early detection of students who have a high potential for violence and extreme behaviors.

In *Best Practice Briefs*, Tableman and Herron (2004) identify procedures to support a safe and orderly environment.

1. Maintain buildings in good physical condition.
2. Reward students for appropriate behavior.
3. Enforce consequences for inappropriate behavior.
4. Use contracts with students to reinforce behavioral expectations.
5. Post behavioral policies on bulletin boards and announce them over public address system at periodic intervals.
6. Initiate anti-bullying, conflict resolution, and peer mediation programs.
7. Engage students, staff, and parents in planning school safety activities and discipline policies.

8. Increase the number of counselors, social workers, and mentors.
9. Create anonymous tip lines or suggestion boxes for reporting dangerous situations or for ideas to improve school climate.
10. Develop strategies, such as structured activities, during lunch periods and passing times.
11. Establish time-out rooms throughout the day.
12. Provide in-school suspension rooms with academic supports.

The National Association of Secondary School Principals (NASSP) provides information focusing on safe schools on its website. Guiding principles and recommendations featured on the NASSP website (www.nassp.org) include:

Schools along with the community, have a shared responsibility to ensure that schools are safe and orderly.

Students and educators have a right to attend schools that have a safe and orderly learning environment.

The NASSP Breaking Ranks framework calls for a personalized learning environment as a condition for student engagement and achievement.

Recommendations for School Leaders

1. School leaders should recognize that it is their responsibility to teach what they expect students to know and be able to do. Teaching appropriate behavior and deterring negative behavior is the responsibility of every staff member.
2. School leaders should create a personalized, warm, safe, orderly, and inviting school environment that includes an adult for every student and one that emphasizes the importance of relationships and shared responsibility for nurturing a healthy, positive school climate.
3. School leaders should develop a uniform code of student conduct that contains clear policies, which are developed with staff and community involvement, fairly and consistently administered, evaluated on a regular basis, and openly communicated to stakeholders. Furthermore, school leaders should make a concerted effort to educate and inform students as to the specifics of the code of conduct as well as expectations for appropriate behavior, and the logical consequences of their behavior.
4. School leadership teams should collect and compile data regarding safety-related incidents and regularly conduct school safety audits, share findings

with staff, students, school partners, and the community, and provide student and staff training for school safety.

5. Schools should develop and continually update emergency preparedness plans that include provisions for responses relating to acts of violence, internal and external threats, weapons, and weapon possession.
6. Schools should implement prevention, intervention, apprehension, and counseling programs to combat negative or violent behavior. This would include conflict resolution and peer mediation programs for both students and staff.

Recommendations for District Leaders

7. School districts should establish violence prevention curriculum, grades K–12.
8. School districts should promote collaboration to ensure continuity and consistent application of policies and practices.
9. School districts should partner with parents, law enforcement, public and private social service agencies, and other agencies to develop programs and services to foster caring schools and communities.
10. School districts should partner with the news media to ensure responsible reporting about school safety issues.
11. Principals' ability to maintain a safe school climate should be as important as their ability to lead instruction and should be evaluated as such.

A Vignette of Best Practice[1]

A middle school in a poor rural district was struggling with both student discipline and academics. The principal displayed little instructional leadership and low state test scores reflected this lack of leadership. Discipline referrals were increasing and the principal showed no interest reversing this trend. Teachers, students, and parents were unhappy with the atmosphere. At the conclusion of the school year, the principal left the district for a position in real estate.

The district hired a veteran teacher at the school to become the new principal. She worked with staff to rewrite the student handbook and discipline code. A positive behavior incentive program was implemented, resulting in reduced discipline referrals. Along with the staff the principal created a brand for the school—AAA or Achievement, Attitude, and Attendance. This became the ongoing mantra and focus of all work in the building. Parent programs were initiated where parents were welcomed into the building to become part of their child's education. Within a year the change in climate and culture turned the school into a place where students, staff, and parents enjoyed attending.

It took many positive changes to forge this new climate environment. Listed below are a few of the programs implemented and supported by this creative new principal.

Students:

Academic All Stars—recognizing student academic success

B.U.G. award—Bringing Up Grades—awarding students for improving their grades. These are students who traditionally receive no academic recognition.

Principal Advisory Council—for student input in school operations

New Student Ambassadors—new students to the building are assigned student mentors to help them assimilate into the culture.

All A awards and assembly

Star Bucks—teachers and staff give students star bucks for positive behavior which go into a drawing for prizes.

Birthday Box—the principal has a box of treats in her office and on a student's birthday he or she goes to the office and picks a treat.

Positive Postcards—sent to parents praising something their child accomplished.

Staff:

Monthly birthday cake—for all those having a birthday that month

Staff Appreciation Week—principal and students do something special for teachers each day.

M &Ms on desk—principal puts an M & M dispenser on her desk for staff

News Articles—principal writes articles in the local paper showcasing teacher activities

All-Star Staff Picture Wall—staff pictures are displayed

Business Cards—principal purchases business cards for all teachers

New Staff Gift—principal provides all new staff with a gift such as a coffee mug, school tee shirt, sweat shirt, or windbreaker

Years of Service Award—recognizing service for 5, 15, and 25 years

A, B, C, D award—*a*bove and *b*eyond the *c*all of *d*uty—recognition for teachers when they do something outside the school day for students

Celebrations:

State Testing Kickoff—treats and focus time for students to prepare for the state academic tests

Festival of Trees—each class decorates a Christmas tree and staff judges the trees and awards a winner

Leaf Raking—students rake leaves one fall day for the elderly in the community

All School Olympics—each grade and staff compete in athletic events—great for school spirit

Family Fun Night—parents and students enjoy food and activities

Breakfast of Champions—parents are invited to school for breakfast as students receive athletic awards

STAR Night—parents are invited to watch their children receive academic awards

Moms and Muffins—moms are invited for muffins and meeting with the principal

Doughnuts and Dads—dads are invited to school in the morning for doughnuts and meeting with the principal

Resources

Technology Applications

The use of Adobe Acrobat workflow software can help to automate recordkeeping, storage, and retention by eliminating file cabinets and allowing access to school information from anywhere, at any time from almost any mobile device. Baeder (2011) offers a long annotated list of *Essential iPad Apps for Principals* including:

- **OmniFocus** to keep track of "countless projects, tasks, ideas, and plans."
- **Evernote** for keeping track of the many random pieces of information that suddenly become available during a principal's day.
- **Numbers** for creating and viewing spreadsheets for budgets and other number-related activities.

Other apps for the iPhone and/or iPad or other mobile devices that are specifically designed or useful for school administrators include:

- **eCove Admin** for gathering both qualitative and quantitative data while observing both teacher and student behavior in the classroom. With the increased emphasis on teacher evaluations, this could become an essential tool in the process. It also is available in a special education edition.
- **TOR** (Teacher Observation Report) for documenting standards-based evaluations to facilitate accurate reflection for teachers and principals in teacher conferences and formal teacher evaluations. Not all states have all of the standardized assessment tools available yet.
- **LawStack** for those times that a principal needs a legal library in his/her pocket.
- **Keynote** and a presentation dangle for creating PowerPoint-like presentations and connecting to an LCD projector for viewing of these presentations by many people without a laptop.
- Direct classroom communication technology via texting, Twitter, or email can also help to minimize teacher/student problems before they become out-of-control crises.
- **Job App Box** for those times when humor is needed to relieve a stressful situation.

For 21st-century principals looking for input and assistance from students and staff to create and maintain an easy-to-access and easy-to-update student and/or school operations manual(s), the creation of a school wiki on the various anticipated issues and behaviors is a good place to begin a shared vision for safe and orderly school operation. A search of the internet will also produce numerous examples of student and school crises manuals from other schools to use to start the discussion on what should be included, but in the end such examples need to be customized to the unique operational environment of the school and its large supporting community. *A Practical Guide for Crisis Response in Our Schools* by the National Center for Crisis Management is a good place for ideas. See http://www.schoolcrisisresponse.com/

Policy for Using Information Technology in School

The following is a policy for technology use from the U.S. Department of Justice (2011) website. The policy is in the public domain so principals may adapt the policy to the conditions in their schools.

The school's information technology resources, including email and internet access, are provided for educational purposes. Adherence to the following policy is necessary for continued access to the school's technological resources:

Students must:

1. *Respect and protect the privacy of others.*
   - Use only assigned accounts.
   - Not view, use, or copy passwords, data, or networks to which they are not authorized.
   - Not distribute private information about others or themselves.

2. *Respect and protect the integrity, availability, and security of all electronic resources.*
   - Observe all network security practices, as posted.
   - Report security risks or violations to a teacher or network administrator.
   - Not destroy or damage data, networks, or other resources that do not belong to them, without clear permission of the owner.
   - Conserve, protect, and share these resources with other students and internet users.

3. *Respect and protect the intellectual property of others.*
   - Not infringe copyrights (no making illegal copies of music, games, or movies!).
   - Not plagiarize.

4. *Respect and practice the principles of community.*
   - Communicate only in ways that are kind and respectful.
   - Report threatening or discomforting materials to a teacher.
   - Not intentionally access, transmit, copy, or create material that violates the school's code of conduct (such as messages that are pornographic, threatening, rude, discriminatory, or meant to harass).
   - Not intentionally access, transmit, copy, or create material that is illegal (such as obscenity, stolen materials, or illegal copies of copyrighted works).

- Not use the resources to further other acts that are criminal or violate the school's code of conduct.
- Not send spam, chain letters, or other mass unsolicited mailings.
- Not buy, sell, advertise, or otherwise conduct business, unless approved as a school project.

Students may, if in accord with the policy above:

1. Design and post web pages and other material from school resources.
2. Use direct communications such as IRC, online chat, or instant messaging with a teacher's permission.
3. Install or download software, if also in conformity with laws and licenses, and under the supervision of a teacher.
4. Use the resources for any educational purpose.

Consequences for Violation. Violations of these rules may result in disciplinary action, including the loss of a student's privileges to use the school's information technology resources.

Supervision and Monitoring. School and network administrators and their authorized employees monitor the use of information technology resources to help ensure that uses are secure and in conformity with this policy. Administrators reserve the right to examine, use, and disclose any data found on the school's information networks in order to further the health, safety, discipline, or security of any student or other person, or to protect property. They may also use this information in disciplinary actions, and will furnish evidence of crime to law enforcement.

I ACKNOWLEDGE AND UNDERSTAND MY OBLIGATIONS:

______________________	______________________
Student	Date
______________________	______________________
Parent/Guardian	Date

I ACKNOWLEDGE AND UNDERSTAND MY OBLIGATIONS:

PARENTS, PLEASE DISCUSS THESE RULES WITH YOUR STUDENT TO ENSURE HE OR SHE UNDERSTANDS THEM.

THESE RULES ALSO PROVIDE A GOOD FRAMEWORK FOR YOUR STUDENT'S USE OF COMPUTERS AT HOME, AT LIBRARIES, OR ANYWHERE.

Instruments Measuring School Climate and School Culture

Many instruments that measure school climate and culture are available to building principals. With these data, principals will have a better understanding of what changes are necessary and whom to involve in that change process in order to promote a more positive school climate and culture. One of the most comprehensive instruments was developed by Victoria Bernhardt (n.d.) and can be found on the Education for the Future website (http://eff.csuchico.edu). These perception surveys assess information from students, staff, and parents, and Education for the Future will analyze the results and even provide graphic detail.

Annotated Bibliography

Bernhardt, V. (n.d.). Assessing perceptions using Education for the Future questionnaires. Education for the Future, Chico, CA, retrieved from http://eff.csuchico.edu. It contains surveys that assist in determining the status of a school's climate.

Cornell, D., & Mayer, M. (2010). Why do school order and safety matter? *Educational Researcher, 39*, 7–15. The lead article in a special issue on school order and safety summarizes the current research on the topic and introduces the other articles in this issue.

Marzano, R. J. (2003). *What works in schools: Translating research into action.* Alexandria, VA: Association of Supervision and Curriculum Development. It introduces school-level, teacher-level, and student-level factors that positively affect student achievement.

Swearer, S., Espelage, D., Vaillancourt, T., & Hymel, S. (2010). What can be done about school bullying? Linking research to educational practice. *Educational Researcher, 39*, 38–47. The article suggests concepts that schools can implement to reduce bullying.

Summary

Parents, students, teachers, and staff all want a safe and orderly place for learning, and principals must understand the culture and climate of the school to determine what changes must be made to achieve it. Elements such as a common vision, shared decision making, publicized and enforced rules, collegiality, high expectations, rewards, celebration, technology supported administrative tools, and safety are all important in developing and maintaining safe and orderly schools. When principals can create an environment in which all the elements of safe and orderly schools exist, research has shown that student achievement increases.

Endnote

1. The vignette was based on a conversation with Mary McCrumb (2011), a middle school principal.

References

Baeder, J. (2011). Essential iPad apps for principals. Retrieved May 18, 2012, from http://www.eduleadership.org/2010/09/01/essential-ipad-apps-for-principals/

Barth, R. (2002). The culture builder. *Educational Leadership, 59*(8), 6–11.

Charlotte Advocates for Education. (2004). *The role of principal leadership in teacher retention.* Retrieved from http://www.advocatesfored.org/principalstudy.htm

Cohen, J., Pickeral, T., & McCloskey, M. (2009). The challenge of assessing school climate. *Educational Leadership, 66*(4).Retrieved from http://www.ascd.org/publications-/educational-leadership/dec08/vol66/num04/The-Challenge-of-Assessing-School-Climate.aspx

Creemers, B. P. M., & Reezigt, G. J. (1999). The role of school and classroom climate in elementary school learning environments. In Freiberg, H.J. (Ed.), *School climate: Measuring, improving and sustaining healthy learning environments* (pp. 30–48). Philadelphia, PA: Falmer.

Deal, T. E., & Peterson, K. D. (2009). *Shaping school culture: Pitfalls, paradoxes, and promises.* New York: Wiley.

DeJung, J., & Duckworth, K. (1986*). High school teachers and their students' attendance: Final Report.* Eugene: University of Oregon Center for Education Policy and Management, College of Education.

Derpak, D., & Yarema, J. (2002). Climate control. *Principal Leadership, 3*(4), 42–45.

Fox, L., & Duda, M. (n.d). *Positive behavior support. Technical Assistance Center on Social and Emotional Intervention for Young Children.* Retrieved from www.challenging behavior.org

Freiberg, H. J. (1998). Measuring school climate: Let me count the ways. *Educational Leadership, 56*(1), p. 22–26.

Glasser, W. (1986). *Control theory in the classroom.* New York: Harper & Row.

Goleman, D. (2006). The socially intelligent leader. *Educational Leadership.* Alexandria, VA: Association for Supervision and Curriculum Development.

Goleman, D., Boyatzis, R., & McKee, A. (2004). *Primal leadership: Learning to lead with emotional intelligence.* Boston: Harvard Business School.

Greene, R. W. (2011). Collaborative problem solving can transform school discipline. *Phi Delta Kappan, 93*(2), 25–28.

Hay Group. (2000). *Raising achievement in our schools: Models of excellence for head-teachers in different settings.* Retrieved from www.ncsl.org.uk/media/F7B/52/kpool-hay-models-of-excellence-parts-1–2.pdf

Hoge, D. R., Smit, E.K., & Hanson, S.L. (1990). School experiences predicting changes in self-esteem of sixth and seventh-grade students. *Journal of Educational Psychology, 82,* 117–127.

Hutton, T., & Bailey, K. (2007). *School policies and legal issues supporting safe schools: Effective strategies for creating safer schools and communities.* The Hamilton Fish Institute on School and Community Violence & Northwest Regional Educational Laboratory. Washington, DC.

Johnson, S. (2009). Improving the school environment to reduce school violence: A review of the literature. *The Journal of School Health, 79*(10), 451–465.

Krajewski, B., & Matkin, M. (1996). Empowering the community: A shared vision, *Principal, 76*(2), 5–8.

Kreft, L. G. G. (1993). Using multilevel analyses to assess school effectiveness: A study of Dutch secondary schools. *Sociology of Education, 66,* 104–129.

Leneway, R. J., & Winters, R. E. (2008). Cyber bullying, part II, The Research, Tech & Learning Educator's ezine. Retrieved from http://www.techlearning.com/article-/cyberbullying-part-2-the-research/44860

Levine, D. U., & Lezotte, L. W. (1995). Effective schools research. In J. A. Banks & C. A. Mcgee Banks (Eds.), *Handbook of research on multicultural education* (pp. 525–547). New York: Macmillan.

Lezotte, L., & McKee, K. (2002). *Assembly required: A continuous school improvement system.* Effective Schools Products. Okemos, MI: Effective Schools Products, Ltd.

Loukas, A. (2007). What is school climate? *Leadership Compass, 5*(1), 1–3. Retrieved from http://www.naesp.org/resources/2/Leadership_Compass/2007/LC2007v5n1a4.pdf

Ma, X. (2001). Bullying and being bullied: To what extent are bullies also victims? *American Educational Research Journal, 38*(2), 351–370.

Marzano, R. J. (2003). *What works in schools: Translating research into action.* Alexandria, VA: Association of Supervision and Curriculum Development.

Marzano, R. J. Mid-continent Research for Education and Learning & Educational Resources Information Center. (2001). *A new era of school reform: Going where the research takes us.* Aurora, CO: Mid-continent Research for Education and Learning.

Marzano, R. J., Waters, T., & McNulty, B. A. (2005). *School leadership that works: From research to results.* Alexandria, VA: Association of Supervision and Curriculum Development.

Maxwell, J. (1998). *The 21 irrefutable laws of leadership: Follow them and people will follow you.* Nashville, TN: Thomas Nelson.

McCrumb, M. (2011). Personal communication.

Miller, S. I., & Fredericks, J. (1990). The false ontology of school climate effects. *Educational Theory, 40*(3), 333–342.

National Association of Secondary School Principals. (2011). *Safe schools.* Retrieved from http://www.nassp.org/Content.aspx?topic=47111

National School Climate Council.(2012). *School climate.* Retrieved from http://www.schoolclimate.org/climate/

Olweus, D. (1993). *Bullying at school: What we know and what we can do.* Oxford: Blackwell.

Perry, A. (1908). *The management of a city school.* New York: Macmillan

Peterson, K. (n.d.). *Shaping school culture. Apple Learning Exchange,* Retrieved from http://ali.apple.com/ali_sites/ali/exhibits/1000488/

Peterson, K., & Deal, T. (2002).*Shaping school culture fieldbook: The heart of leadership.* San Francisco, CA: Jossey-Bass.

Peterson, K. D., & Deal, T. E. (1998). How leaders influence the culture of schools. *Educational Leadership, 56*(1), 28–30.

Phillips, G. (1996). *Classroom rituals for at-risk learners.* Vancouver, BC: Educserv, British Columbia School Trustees.

Rauhauser, W., & McLennan, A. (1995). *America's schools: Making them work.* Chapel Hill, NC: New View.

Robbins, S. (2002). *The difference between managing and leading: Understanding people will help you make the shift from managing to leading a business.* Retrieved from http://www.entrepreneur.com/article/57304

Rumberger, R.W. (1987). High school dropouts: A review of issues and evidence. *Review of Educational Research, 57,* 101–121.

Saphier, J., & King, M. (1985). Good seeds grow in strong cultures. *Educational Leadership, 42*(6), 67–74.

Searcy, N., Hall, C., & Edwards, K. (2000). The work of leadership, part 2. Retrieved from http://www.smartleadership.com/article_current.html

Selznick, P. (1957). *Leadership in administration: A sociological interpretation.* Evanston, IL: Row, Peterson.

Sommer, B. (1985). What's different about truants? A comparison study of eighth graders. *Journal of Youth and Adolescence, 14,* 411–422.

Tableman, B., & Herron, A. (2004). School climate and learning. *Best Practice Briefs, 31.* East Lansing, MI: Michigan State University. Retrieved from http://outreach.msu.edu/bpbriefs/issues/brief31.pdf

Ubben, G., Hughes, L., & Norris, C. (2010). *The principal: Creative leadership for excellence in schools* (7th ed). Englewood Cliffs, NJ: Prentice-Hall.

U.S. Department of Justice. (2011). *A model acceptable use policy for schools.* Retrieved from http://www.justice.gov/criminal/cybercrime/rules/acceptableUsePolicy.htm

Wagner, C. R., & Hall-O'Phelan, M. (1998). *Improving schools through the administration and analysis of school culture audits.* Paper presented at the Mid-South Educational Research Association, New Orleans, LA.

Walker, H. (1995). Preventing violence in schools. *Research Roundup, 11*(2), 2–5.

Wu, S., Pink, W., Crain, R., & Moles, O. (1982). Student suspension: A critical reappraisal. *The Urban Review, 14*(4), 245–303.

4

High, Cohesive, and Culturally Relevant Expectations for All Students

GARY L. WEGENKE AND SUE POPPINK

Introduction

How to serve the needs of *all* students has long been a concern of educators, and, for more than half a century, federal policy makers. Federal legislation and court cases have mandated that schools improve the learning opportunities for all students, including students with disabilities, students from economically disadvantaged backgrounds, students in need of having their civil rights protected, and others.

Today nearly all public schools are influenced by the No Child Left Behind Act of 2001 (NCLB, 2002). The expectation is that schools will pursue courses of action to increase student proficiency in reading and math as well as close racial and socioeconomic achievement gaps.

As school leaders struggle to serve these federal mandates, the demographics of America, including school-aged children, continue to change. Banks (1999) predicted by 2020, our nation's schools would have half of their student population represented by students of color. Additionally, public opinion is focused on educating *all* students to be able upon graduation to compete in a global-knowledge-based economy.

The Importance of Mission, Culture, Climate, and Goals

Organizations, including national and international school systems, are focusing on creating missions, visions, goals, and structures to improve the academic performance of their students. The spotlight for accomplishing high expectations is on school leaders—principals and teachers. Specifically, the principal's leadership ability and skills to adapt and influence processes linked to instruction and learning make a difference (Hallinger & Heck, 1996; Waters, Marzano, & McNulty, 2004).

The future is not just a place we are all going but a place we are creating, which becomes the North Star for school principals. To improve the learning opportunities for all children, principals might consider the importance of reshaping their school's culture to reflect the community's culture. Sergiovanni (1999, p. 11) defines "school culture as the values, beliefs, symbols, and shared meanings of parents, teachers, and interested others within the community." "The culture of a group," according to Schein (1997, p. 12), "is a pattern of shared basic assumptions that the group learned as it solved problems of external adaption and internal integration. . . ." Utilizing these definitions of culture, skilled principals may begin their work of increasing student performance by creating a clear statement of school mission that reflects the school's culture. The school's mission clarifies the conditions under which decisions will be made. Cotton (2003, p. 10) acknowledged that a "study of . . . 24 schools found that in the successful schools, principals and other school leaders talked enthusiastically and engagingly about what the school stands for. . . ." Robert Terry, in *Authentic Leadership,* implied that a strong mission statement will enable an organization to envision a variety of ways to pursue success.

Another avenue for the school principal to explore is to come to an understanding of the importance of school climate. Culture is the implicit way in which schools work; climate is a reading of how members of an organization feel about the organization. Sergiovanni and Starratt (1998, p. 177) suggested that "climate provides a reading of how things are going in the school and a basis for predicting school consequences and outcomes." Understanding school climate is a step toward reshaping a school's culture.

Setting goals focused on high standards for student success may lead to a healthy school climate and culture. Lunenburg and Ornstein (2000, p. 72) explained, "a healthy school is characterized by student and teacher behavior that is harmonious and works toward instructional success." As the instructional leader, the principal's job is to engage other stakeholders in a goal-setting process by first determining: (1) What are we doing? (2) Why are we doing what we are doing? (3) How are we going to achieve our desired outcomes? and (4) Are there alternative ways to achieve those outcomes? In responding to these questions, the process should guide stakeholders toward establishing shared goals and ultimately action plans. Ubben and Hughes (1997, p. 24) stated that "people will work hard to achieve goals they helped develop."

The Importance of High Expectations Standards

Evaluations of programs aimed at preventing students from academic failure and dropping out of school have demonstrated that a student's relationship with significant people (i.e., principals, teachers, parents) makes a difference, particularly if those significant people have "high expectations." All students, including students from low-income backgrounds, need an advocate who believes in their ability to succeed. Some factors appearing to convey high expectations and hope to students are (1) personal relationships expressing the thought "I won't give up on you," (2) respect in the form of recognized strengths, and (3) academic work built on the interests and strengths of the student.

Finally, a relationship conveying high expectations requires an awareness of the extent to which students believe in their own skills and abilities. By developing an I-can-achieve attitude, students take responsibility for their own learning and become resilient, knowing they are first, capable of achieving in school and second, of raising their own levels of academic success.

For the most part, principals have an indirect influence on student achievement and performance. However, teachers and parents have a direct role in influencing the success of students. Manthey (2006, p. 23) explained, "When teachers believe they can positively affect student achievement, schools may be able to succeed when it had been thought impossible." The collective efficacy beliefs of teachers within a school are a probable link between what teachers perceive about their colleagues' instructional skills and abilities and the degree to which students perform and achieve.

The Importance of Collaborative Decision Making with Parents and Guardians

Collaborative decision making and problem solving are important means to consider when approaching the day-to-day routines of effective schools. The collective belief is a commitment that what takes place within the school makes a difference in the instructional practices of teachers and student achievement. The principal has a responsibility to structure each day "to ensure that collaboration around instructional issues becomes an important part of the school day and school week" (Cotton, 2003, p. 23).

Collaborative activities go beyond the school's doors. Demmert (2001) supported the concept that principals and teachers build trust and partnerships with families when they encourage parents to be involved in their children's formal schooling. Historically, some parents of urban school children did not have a good experience in school. Lunenburg and Ornstein (2000, p. 203) present a case for parent involvement by saying, " . . . parents, especially the urban poor who were not successful in school are disenfranchised stakeholders in the educational system . . . [they] need non-threatening interactions with educators." The principal's responsibility in re-shaping school culture is, in part, collaborating with parents, knowing they are the child's first and primary teachers. Successful principals develop positive relationships with parents by managing differences—differences related to parents' cultural backgrounds, beliefs, and norms.

Leithwood and Jantzi (1999) conducted a research study related to leadership sources and their effects on students' engagement with school. One of the findings was that family culture was significant, the assumption being that school leaders need parents and parents need school leaders if students are to stay engaged with their own schooling.

The Importance of Cultural Competence

"Cultural competence is the ability to successfully teach students from cultures other than our own" (Ming & Dukes, 2006, p. 42). To be effective cultural competence must become an integral factor in a school's renewal process. Cultural competence is a developmental process which takes place at the individual, group, and school system levels.

Individuals and leaders who are considered culturally competent are able to adapt to different cultural beliefs and practices as well as understand their own cultural views. Schools desiring to be culturally competent must develop a clearly stated vision related to the importance of inclusiveness and student performance.

Principals and teachers are constantly working with students whose ethnic, cultural, linguistic, racial, and socioeconomic backgrounds are different than their own. Culturally relevant teaching "uses student cultures in order to maintain it and to transcend the negative effects of the dominant culture" (Ladson-Billings, 1994, p. 17). Ladson-Billings goes on to say, "Specifically, culturally relevant teaching, that is, a pedagogy that empowers students intellectually, socially, emotionally and politically by using cultural referents to impart knowledge, skills and attitudes" (p. 18).

A challenge facing school principals and classroom teachers wherever they are located is that classroom norms remain embedded in the values and expectations associated with Western European culture. For this reason, becoming culturally responsive may allow teachers, as well as principals, to proactively address high expectations for all students in terms of academic performance and achievement.

Research on High, Cohesive, and Culturally Relevant Expectations for Students

Setting the Stage for Research on Teacher and Parent Expectations

Rosenthal and Jacobson's *Pygmalion in the Classroom* (1968), which argued that students respond to teachers' "self-fulfilling prophecy" in terms of classroom learning, created a stir in the education community concerning teacher expectations (Proctor, 1984). In the study, teachers of an experimental group of students were told that children had obtained high scores on a test that meant they were poised for "blooming." Those students were expected to show a significant increase in intellectual competence. In fact, those children were part of a randomly selected experimental group which showed no particular reason for them to excel. Students were re-administered the test eight months later, and they showed significantly greater gains in total IQ than a control group did. Rosenthal and Jacobson argued the existence of a "self-fulfilling prophecy bias" that led to teachers' differential treatment of the experimental children. This work has been severely criticized on methodology grounds (Barber, 1973; Snow, 1969; Thorndike, 1968).

While the methodology of Rosenthal and Jacobson had been criticized, multiple studies since that time have shown that teacher expectations matter (Brophy, 1982; Proctor, 1984). The research on teacher expectations continues to expand (Rist, 2000).

Literature on Teacher and Parent Expectations

The literature on the role of teacher expectations is large and complex, as researchers have looked at the role of students' expectations and demographic information, parental expectations and demographic information, school context, and other related ideas. Often research has centered on teachers' perceptions of low-income and African American students' academic capacity (Farkas, 2003). But students from nearly every demographic, including immigrant children, have been studied.

In addition, early on, Brophy and Good (1974) developed a model of teacher expectations. And later, Brophy focused on (1) the appropriateness of differential teacher expectations and teacher–student interaction patterns, (2) the role of individual differences in teachers, (3) conceptualizing the self-fulfilling prophecy effects in classrooms, (4) the role of individual differences in students, and (5) implications for teaching and teacher education.

Marzano (2003) found the act of setting academic goals for classrooms had an effect size of 0.55 (Marzano, 2003, p. 35), which means that the achievement scores in classes where clear learning goals were exhibited were 0.55 standard deviations higher than the achievement scores for classes where clear learning goals were not established; which translates into a 21-percentage difference in achievement.

Research on parents' expectations has found that they interact with others' expectations (such as their children's) and their children's experiences in schools. For instance, "high levels of parent–child interactions increase parents' and children's expectations and . . . higher shared family expectations enhance achievement and greater differences suppress achievement" (Hao & Bonstead-Bruns, 1998 p. 98). Native American, American-born, and immigrants' parents' expectations for their students have also been explored (Goldenberg, Gallimore, Reese & Garnier, 2001; Hao & Bonstead-Bruns, 1998). For instance, Goldenberg, Gallimore, Reese, and Garnier (2001) found that Latino immigrant parents' aspirations are high, but their expectations are influenced by their child's performance in school.

Cohesive Expectations

The expectations of schools as a collective have also been an intense area of study since the Rosenthal and Jacobson paper. Brookover and his colleagues found as early as 1979 that school climate, as measured by a variable referred to as "Student Sense of Academic Futility," has a strong correlation with achievement. Their work also made suggestions about the processes through which climate affects achievement.

In 1989, Newmann, Rutter, and Smith studied the organizational factors that affect school sense of efficacy, community, and expectations and found that the most powerful organizational effects were "students' orderly behavior, the encouragement of innovation, teachers' knowledge of one another's courses, the responsiveness of administrators and teachers' helping one another" (p. 221).

Weinstein, Madison, and Kuklinski (1995) argued that the context in which teachers work can influence their (1) thinking about students' abilities and teacher efficacy, their (2) need to keep issues of improving teaching private, and, with administrators and their (3) lack of support for collaborative action and for mixed-ability grouping in schools. In working together to change the context, teachers, administrators, and researchers were able to increase student learning opportunities.

Schools in Chicago under site-based management needed (1) higher teacher expectations for students, (2) the opportunity for schools to do things differently including additional resources, and (3) the capacity of teachers to dramatically improve the level of instruction. But beyond school-based management accountability was needed. Accountability was needed to "address the lack of will among school staffs to undertake change and among students to be highly engaged in learning" (Hess, 1999).

Goddard, Hoy, and Hoy (2000, 2004) have conducted a number of studies on collective teacher efficacy, in which they've found that when teachers collectively hold high expectations for students—part of teachers' collective efficacy—students' achievement is higher.

Diamond, Randolph, and Spillane (2004, p. 75) also looked at school expectations through a lens of "organizational habitus" and found that the "concentration of low-income African American students in urban elementary schools is deeply coupled with a leveling of teachers' expectations of students and a reduction in their sense of responsibility for student learning. This process is rooted in school-based organizational habitus through which expectations for students become embedded in schools." Furthermore, they found that school leaders can have a strong influence. They stated that one way to raise expectations for students is for "school leaders to engage in practices designed to increase teachers' sense of responsibility."

Culturally Relevant Expectations

In the 1980s, the educational anthropology literature exploded with a focus on Culturally Responsive Schooling (CRS); (called by a number of different names; see, e.g., Brown, 1980; Deyhle, 1992; Greenbaum & Greenbaum, 1983; McLaughlin, 1989). This scholarship, combined with related work in the fields of education and multicultural education, seemed to bring the discussion of CRS into the mainstream. Furthermore, the rapidly increasing racial and ethnic diversity among youth in U.S. schools in the 1980s and 1990s also resulted in an increased interest in CRS among a wide array of educators. Scholarship from disciplines as diverse as anthropology, psychology, applied linguistics, and sociology added to the growing body of knowledge about the challenges minority students were facing in schools. As Pewewardy and Hammer (2003) note, "much was learned about student motivation, power relations, and resistance . . . ; language and cognition . . .; culture and cognition . . . ; and motivation and learning styles . . . , to mention only a small sample of this body of work" (p. 1).

Though culturally responsive schooling has been advocated for over 40 years, it has had little impact on teachers because there is little in the way of systemic, institutional, or lasting changes to schools serving indigenous youth (Castagno & Brayboy, 2008).

Certain methods of teaching, such as using action words and employing the communal approach (rather than the individualistic approach), are more effective for African American children than for white children (Boykin & Cunningham, 2001; Dill & Boykin, 2000), and thus, culturally-relevant pedagogy (Ladson-Billings, 1994, 1995a, 1995b, 1998).

Models and Best Practices for Creating High, Cohesive, and Culturally Relevant Expectations for Students

In schools with adults who have high expectations for students, students experience academic growth. The schools' cultures and the community's cultures including values, beliefs, and expectations for their children are significant if schools are to progress and succeed. Selected models and best practices for creating and maintaining high, cohesive, and culturally relevant expectations for students within schools are presented.

High Expectations: A Question of Mission

Robert Terry, in *Authentic Leadership* (1993), suggested that the ability of an organizational leader (the school principal) to frame "human action" issues correctly is essential if the issues are to be resolved. He projected a theory that connects parts of his model (the Terry Model) that can be used as a "tool" to generate new ways to look at issues. The model contains a diamond with four connected points leaders need to address—"mission," "power," "structures," and "resources" bound together within community (see Figure 4.1).

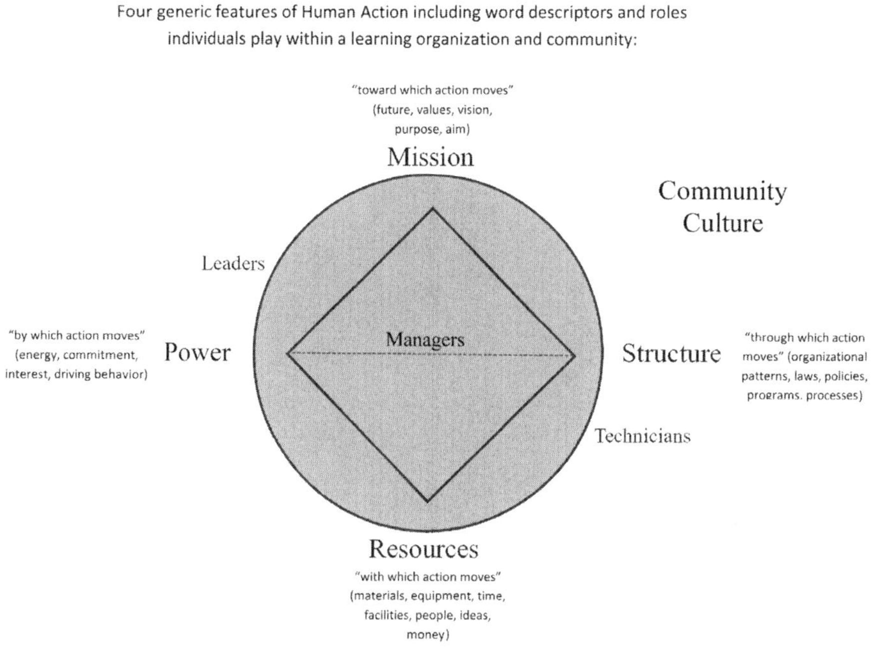

Four generic features of Human Action including word descriptors and roles individuals play within a learning organization and community:

"toward which action moves" (future, values, vision, purpose, aim)

Mission

Community Culture

Leaders

"by which action moves" (energy, commitment, interest, driving behavior)

Power

Managers

Structure

"through which action moves" (organizational patterns, laws, policies, programs. processes)

Technicians

Resources

"with which action moves" (materials, equipment, time, facilities, people, ideas, money)

Figure 4.1 Human Action Within Community Culture

*Adapted, with permission, from Terry's (1993) *Authentic Leadership.*

Terry describes "mission" (directs, gives purpose to), "power" (energizes, drives behavior), "structure" (laws, policies, programs) and "resources" (people, dollars, etc.) as constructs through which human action moves. The "community" gives meaning to the organization, explaining why the organization exists. Terry also explains that "leaders" conduct their work between mission and power whereas "managers" perform their roles between power and structures. "Technicians" find themselves operating between structure and resources. A final comment would be that organizations (e.g., schools) driven by their missions will enable and empower school stakeholders to create their own vision statements, taking responsibility for setting goals of common interest. In contrast, school organizations driven by resources and their allocations will continually be limited in achieving their missions and visions.

High Expectations: A Question of School Leadership

Figure 4.2 represents a School-Based Leadership Model developed and implemented by the superintendent of schools and other stakeholders within the Des Moines (IA) Community School District (1988 to 1998). The model reflected the importance of leadership at the building level if "high cohesive expectations," were to become a reality for the district's 33,000 students. Once the district's mission was made policy—a focus on student learning and success for all students—the central staff was placed in roles of supporting the district's principals and their schools. The principal's role as a visionary, facilitator, and instructional leader was paramount to student success on 60 school sites.

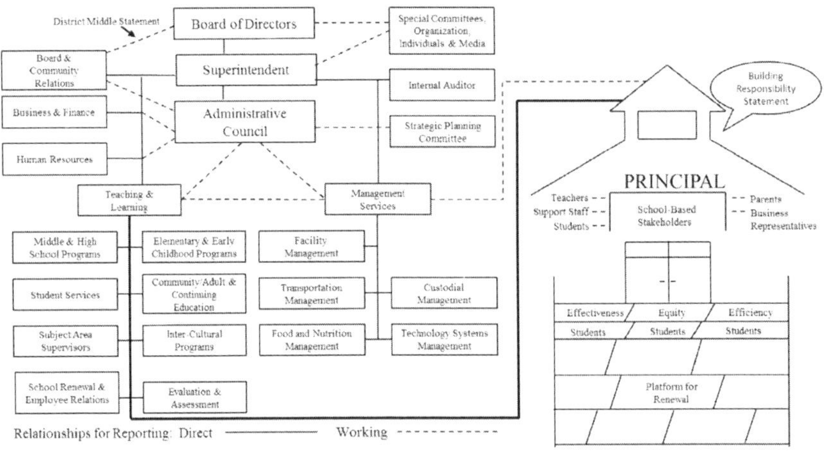

Figure 4.2 School-based Leadership with a Focus on Interdependence

The model (Figure 4.3) reflects the importance of building responsibility (vision) statements being in accord with the school district's mission statement. School issues related to serving *all* students are *effective* (student performance), *equitable* (student inclusiveness), and *efficient* (instructional delivery). The three components are major foci of school-based goal setting and action planning and implementation.

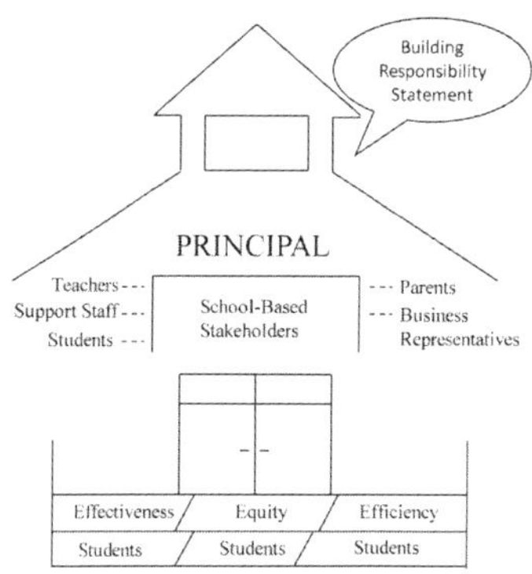

School-Based Councils

- Build Understanding
- Create Communication Links
- Design School Improvement Plan
- Involved with "How" Instruction is Delivered
- Involved with Resource Allocation
- Emphasis on Consensus Building
- Focus on Results

Education Tools

- Building Data Bases
  - √ Demographic Information
  - √ Effective School Information
  - √ Test Result Information
  - √ Discipline, Attendance, Dropout Information
- Allocating Resources
  - √ Decentralized Budgets
  - √ Staffing Formulas
- District Policies and Procedures
- State Instructional Standards

Focal Points for an "Effective" School

- Understand that
  - Students come in all sizes and shapes
  - Parents send the best children they have to school.
- Success Keys:
  - Effectiveness, Equity, and Efficiency
- Educational Tools
  - Data
  - Professional Development
- "Building Responsibility Statement"
- School-Based Councils

Figure 4.3 School-Level Goal Setting

School-based councils to monitor and promote student progress and school success were an integral part of the school-based leadership process. Educational tools were to be used to "improve" the student bodies' progress rather than "prove" that students were not progressing. The statement that "what gets monitored gets done" came to life in the Des Moines Community School District over the 10-year period.

High Expectations: A Question of Parental Involvement

In *The Superintendent's Fieldbook,* N. Cambron-McCabe et al. (2005) cite seven principles or best practices for involving parents in their children's schooling:

1. *Parents are the most important persons to the child.* To ensure the health and well-being of children, assure the well-being of parents.
2. *Parents are your partners.* Parents are partners who work on behalf of the child. The relationship with them is predicated on equality and respect.

3. *Parents are their own best advocates.* Consider parents as decision makers on a collaborative team. Listen to and give parents choices when working with their children.
4. *Parents are assets.* Parents aren't the problem. They're not a barrier to overcome, but rather an asset to work with their child. Build on parents' strengths and what they can do to help their child.
5. *When working with parents, make school programs relevant and community based.* Parents are often more comfortable working with their child in a community context.
6. *Parent volunteerism is a good thing.* Avoid compelling parents to work with the school, but allow them opportunities to volunteer.
7. *Parents want to be productive.* Self-esteem, joy, and hopefulness are important for building strong ties between the school and groups of parents.

High Expectations: A Question of Professional Ethics

In 1996, the Interstate School Leaders Licensure Consortium (ISLLC) encouraged the development of six standards for school leaders that assert that school leadership is complex and multi-faceted. Owings, Kaplan, and Nunnery (2002) state that, "effective leaders often espouse different patterns of beliefs and act differently from the norm in the profession" (p. 5). Principals interested in effective school leadership issues are encouraged to use the ISLLC Standards as a total package. The six standards are:

Standard 1

A school administrator is an educational leader who promotes the success of all students by facilitating the development, articulation, implementation, and stewardship of a vision of learning that is shared and supported by the school community.

Standard 2

A school administrator is an educational leader who promotes the success of all students by advocating, nurturing, and sustaining a school culture and instructional program conducive to student learning and staff professional growth.

Standard 3

A school administrator is an educational leader who promotes the success of all students by ensuring management of the organization, operations, and resources for a safe, efficient, and effective learning environment.

Standard 4

A school administrator is an educational leader who promotes the success of all students by collaborating with families and community members, responding to diverse community interests and needs, and mobilizing community resources.

Standard 5

A school administrator is an educational leader who promotes the success of all students by acting with integrity, fairness, and in an ethical manner.

Standard 6

A school administrator is an educational leader who promotes the success of all students by understanding, responding to, and influencing the larger political, social, economic, legal, and cultural context.

Mechanisms Related to Setting High, Cohesive, and Culturally Relevant Expectations for Students

School principals need to develop a sense of where and how to focus their attention on factors that impact student success. The role principals can play in narrowing the student achievement gap provides a framework to address selected factors such as (1) instructional leadership, (2) culture and school climate, (3) school mission and vision, (4) teacher collaboration and efficacy/collective responsibility, (5) engaging parents and communication, and (6) cultural competence and culturally relevant pedagogy.

The Principal's Leadership

The importance of the school's principal being identified as an "instructional leader" has been suggested for several decades in educational literature.

The early research of Brookover et al. (1979) and Edmonds (1979) asked "What are the distinguishing factors that differentiate high and low performing schools?" Their investigation supported their effective schools research with correlates that include (1) strong (general) leadership by the principal, (2) high expectations for students and staff, (3) a safe and orderly environment, (4) a focus on student learning, (5) regular monitoring of student achievement, (6) resources focused on achievement objectives, and (7) instructional leadership by the principal.

These seven correlates of an effective school provide guidelines for principals to renew and transform their schools by facilitating processes leading to student academic success for all students. With the spotlight on principals' capacity to initiate instructional leadership activities, principals' roles and behaviors became of interest to educational researchers.

According to Cotton (2003), the emphasis on results moved reform to a new level of accountability. The shift from schools designing and implementing effective programs has given way to the public's demand for schools to improve students' academic achievement. Cotton's research on principals of successful schools is illustrated by 26 principals' behaviors that contribute to student achievement. These behaviors fell into five areas of concern: (1) establishing a clear focus on student learning, (2) interactions and relationships, (3) school culture, (4) instruction, and (5) accountability. Cotton's research emphasized that a principal's strong focus on academics was a key determinant of achievement outcomes. Principals of high-achieving schools, in cooperation with those having a stake in the school, need to establish a vision and goals directed at high levels of student learning. Principals need to communicate to stakeholders the importance of high expectations for all students that are in accord with reshaping school culture in support of the schools' goals. The allocation of generous amounts of time to core subject objectives, vision statements, and an emphasis on the school's academic goals are the principal's responsibility. Cotton recognized the principal's evaluation of all change proposals in terms of student learning as part of the vision that guides high-achieving schools. According to Cotton's research successful schools that are focused on high expectations reflect the natural tendency of all children to perform at high levels when "high performance is not based on pushing children, but on . . . facilitating conditions that deliver learning in a way that fits . . . engages and energizes the child" (Butler, as cited in Cotton, p. 12).

Hallinger and Heck (1996) reviewed 40 empirical studies produced from 1980 to 1995. They found the principal's ability to adapt and influence internal processes linked to student learning was important. These internal processes include (1) setting academic expectations, (2) establishing a school mission and goals, (3) identifying student learning opportunities, and (4) protecting instructional time.

Heck (1992) asked the question, "What are the most important instructional leadership predictors of school achievement?" He examined data from 31 elementary and 25 high schools in California in a study that focused on the principal as well as the classroom behaviors of teachers. The study supported the belief that the principal's instructional leadership could predict student achievement based on the amount of time principals spend (1) directly observing classroom practices, (2) promoting discussion about instructional issues, and (3) emphasizing the use of test results.

Culture and School Climate

Context plays an important role in deciding whether a principal selects one leadership approach over another. What school leaders say and do most often is a result of how they interpret the culture.

Leithwood and Jantzi (1999) studied the effects of principals' and teachers' sources of leadership on students' engagement with schools, the school conditions mediating such leadership, and the moderating effects of family culture. The results indicated that if students are engaged with the school, it is likely that the school will be able to influence them. This happens when principals and teachers engage students in meaningful academic classroom and out-of-class instructional activities. A significant finding was that the family's educational culture was related to their children's engagement with school. Obviously, partnerships with families need to be encouraged and implemented if students are to stay in school.

DiGiorgio (2008) studied the principal's role in maintaining a growing minority language school while implementing an inclusive policy for students with learning and physical difficulties. Maintaining a distinct identity was a defining part of a school's success. DiGiorgio examination of policies and practices regarding language, ability grouping, and the school's resource teaching model led to the conclusion principals can shape the "inclusive" and "exclusive" environment of a school.

Shared Vision and Goals

"Leaders move people from selfish concerns to serving the common good. This requires vision and the ability to guide people toward it" (Pinchot, 1996, p. 25).

Different perspectives are held by practicing school leaders and educational researchers regarding ways that school principals influence student outcomes. Witziers, Bosker, and Kruger (2003) examined a list of principal leadership behaviors, including (1) defining and communicating the mission, (2) supervising and evaluating the curriculum, (3) monitoring student progress, (4) coordinating and managing curriculum, (5) being visible, (6) promoting school improvement and professional development, and (7) maintaining an achievement orientation. Following a meta-analysis for each sub-dimension they found that "defining and communicating mission seems to be the most relevant leadership behavior in terms of improving student outcomes . . ." (p. 410).

Terry (1993) explained that "missions, be they small or large, direct and focus power. The value of an organization's mission is judged by the significance of its related meaning" (p. 84). Mission statements define the fundamental purpose of a school; providing a snapshot of where the school desires to be in the future. School mission statements should be a result of engagement with stakeholders in a planned process to determine what beliefs, values, and dreams they have in common.

A mission statement can be further refined into a vision statement that is also a source of inspiration, providing criteria (goals and objectives) to assist in the determination of student academic progress and success. Sergiovanni (1999) supports the concept of "purposing" which aligns with "visioning" as a tool that provides clarity, consensus, and commitment regarding an organization's purpose. "Purposing is a powerful force that responds to human needs for a sense of what is important and a signal of what is of value." Most important, "when a school vision embodies the sharing of ideals, a covenant is created that bonds together leaders to lead in fulfilling a common cause" (p. 86).

"To arrive at a shared vision . . . listen closely for the cherished dreams that staff and community hold" (Deal & Peterson, 1990, p. 200). This statement implies that school principals as "visionary leaders" are continually communicating school system missions aligned with statements of vision. To create a shared vision that motivates all stakeholders, principals must be "visible" in school and community life, and be constantly probing for "latent sentiments, values and expectations . . . and bring these to the front for public discussion, consideration and enactment."

Pounder, Ogawa, and Adams (1995) examined the relationship between the leadership exerted by principals, teachers, office assistants, and parents; four functions of effective organizations; and several measures of school effectiveness. The results showed that the leadership of principals and teachers was positively related to organizational commitment. In turn, commitment was positively related to the perception of the effectiveness of schools. Of note, the leadership of parents was positively associated with student achievement.

Instructional Leadership

O'Donnell and White (2005) selected Pennsylvania public middle schools in which to identify significant relationships between the principal's instructional leadership behaviors and student achievement with school socioeconomic status (SES). Using Hallinger and Murphy's (1987) *Principal Instructional Management Scale (PIMRS)* to measure faculty and principal perceptions; they made two significant findings related to the principal's leadership ability in (1) promoting the school's learning climate and (2) defining the school's mission. Principals who are seeking to become effective instructional leaders should note that framing schools goals and communicating school goals are important activities. Developing and sustaining a "shared vision" with "attainable goals" should result ina school environment "where trust is felt . . . risk can occur with high levels of comfort . . . and teachers . . . become followers" (p. 68).

Teacher Organization and Efficacy

Education revolves around the instructional work, in and outside the classroom, of teachers. Student achievement and school success are possible when faculties collaborate, support, and learn from their peers and believe collectively they have the capacity to impact student learning and achievement.

Goddard's (2001) research applied a theoretical analysis that discussed social cognitive theory at the "group level" to explain the formation and impact of "collective efficacy." Collective efficacy is defined as the capability of teachers to work to achieve a desired result. Specifically, Goddard commented, "[collective efficacy] is analogous to self-efficacy . . . associated with the tasks, level of effort, persistence, thoughts, stress levels and achievement of groups" (p. 467). Little research has been done on collective efficacy.

Assuming teacher self-efficacy is associated with productive teacher behaviors that foster student achievement, Goddard asked, "Is collective efficacy similarly related to differences between schools in student achievement?" (p. 468). He found that what teachers collectively believe about the past achievement of their school influences their perceptions of the effectiveness of their school.

Lee and Smith's (1996) research investigated how the organization of teachers' work affects students in their early years of high school. Teachers' work involved (1) collective responsibility for teacher learning, (2) staff cooperation, and (3) control over classroom and school work conditions. The results were consistent in all three areas studied. Student achievement gains were significantly higher, implying that teacher work defined by *collaboration, cooperation, and sharing* information regarding student achievement does make a case for collective efficacy to be used as a construct for school renewal.

Goddard, Hoy, and Hoy (2004) synthesized existing research on how teachers' practice and student learning are affected by perceptions of collective efficacy. Their findings indicated that:

1. "Mastery experience" is the most significant source of "self-efficacy" for a teacher. The teacher's perception is that past successful performances tend to raise future efficacy (capability) beliefs.
2. "Sense of efficacy" is a significant predictor of productive teaching practices. Trust in one's ability to affect student achievement is the first step toward establishing "collective efficacy" within a school.
3. The higher teachers' sense of "self-efficacy," the more likely they are to take on and overcome difficult tasks, innovate in the teaching and learning process, and network with other teachers to accomplish desired goals.
4. Schools' culture of perceived "collective efficacy" may exert a strong influence on teachers' self-efficacy for instruction and indirectly influence student achievement.

Cultural Competence

Much of the research linking cultural competence and cultural responsive practice to student achievement is not definitive or beneficial to urban school leaders seeking guidance on how to increase student test scores. However, school leaders—principals—will find studies that demonstrate how understanding and practicing cultural responsiveness does affect achievement for culturally rich student bodies.

Ladson-Billings (1995a) examined the teaching practices of eight exemplary teachers of African American students. The eight case studies provided a means to reflect on practices that define and recognize culturally relevant teaching (CRT). Ladson-Billings' literature review found common features as to "why" disconnects occur between students' home's and community cultures and school classrooms. The features were (1) speech and language interaction patterns of teachers and students, (2) student achievement success occurs in social structures outside of school, and (3) "cultural congruence" with the school's "mainstream" culture leading to mere accommodation of a student's cultures within the classroom. Ladson-Billings suggests the term "culturally responsive" refers to a more synergistic relationship between home/community culture and school culture.

According to Ladson-Billings, "culturally responsive" pedagogy used by teachers in the classrooms studied did result in students achieving. Academic achievement was not limited to standardized assessments. Students demonstrated their abilities to reach, write, speak, compute, and pose and solve problems. According to Ladson-Billings, culturally relevant teaching must meet three criteria: (1) an ability to develop students academically, (2) the willingness to nurture and support cultural competence, and (3) the development of a critical consciousness.

Boykin and Cunningham (2001) examined the effects on performance of incorporating cultural factors into the presentation and content of task materials. The researchers listened to stories read to 64 low-income African American elementary students. Two different learning contexts were used in the study—first, a context where music and movement opportunities were provided (High Movement Expressive) and, second, a context where no music and movement opportunities were offered (Low Movement Expressive). The African American children's overall performance was significantly better under the High Movement Expressive conditions. The conclusion was that this study, like previous studies, supports the finding that "facilitative" effects of incorporating music and movement on African American children's cognitive reasoning performance "make a difference" (p. 80). Motivation, achievement factors, and performance are often overlooked when at odds with "mainstream" learning contexts. However, Dill and Boykin (2000) recognize that High Movement Expressiveness ties a student's home culture together with his or her school culture, which, in turn, facilitates student learning.

Castagno and Brayboy (2008) reviewed the literature on culturally responsive schooling (CRS) for indigenous youth, specifically American Indian and Alaskan Native students. Castagno and Brayboy stated "a firm grounding in the heritage language and language indigenous to a particular tribe is a fundamental pre-requisite for the development of culturally healthy students and their communities" (p. 941).

A challenge for creating culturally responsive schooling in today's schools is the emphasis on standardization and high stakes accountability issues (i.e., the No Child Left Behind Act of 2001). Castagno and Brayboy suggested that much is written on CRS; however, it has little impact on what actually takes place in classrooms because teachers must teach the "essentials," which does not result in "systemic" change to schools. One of their observations is, " . . . students of color and students from low-income backgrounds consistently . . . perform lower than their peers according to traditional measures of achievement because their home culture is at odds with the culture and expectations of schools" (p. 946). Education, tribal sovereignty, and self-determination are very important to American Indian and Native Alaskan youth but are rarely recognized by mainstream educators. The racism that indigenous youth must endure in our nation's schools has an impact on student achievement. Finally, Castagno and Brayboy suggest educators must develop some understanding of epistemological concerns "because one's epistemology is fundamental to how he or she sees the world, understands knowledge and lives and negotiates everyday experiences" (p. 952).

Conclusion

High, cohesive, and culturally relevant expectations for *all* students are more than a desirable concept. The future of America is dependent on the academic progress and success of *all* students from pre-K through advanced schooling. Careful reflective thought, planning, and school renewal actions taken by school leaders are an excellent ways to begin this important process.

An Annotated Bibliography of Suggested Readings and Tools

Cambron-McCabe, N., Cunningham, L. L., Harvey, J., & Koff, R. H. (2005). *The superintendent's fieldbook. A guide for leaders of learning.* Thousand Oaks, CA: Corwin Press. This fieldbook is a reference for all school leaders who desire to improve the learning processes within their system. Topics of interest include coping with governance challenges, developing your principals, understanding race and class, engaging your community, and collaborating with your allies.

Cotton, K. (2003). *Principals and student achievement: What the research says.* Alexandria, VA: Association for Supervision and Curriculum Development. The author establishes that goals focused on high levels of student learning and high expectations of students, among other factors, are related to higher student achievement.

Goddard, R. D., Hoy, W. K., & Hoy, A. W. (2004). Collective efficacy beliefs, theoretical developments, empirical evidence, and future directions. *Educational Researcher, 33*(3), 3–13. The authors reviewed research on how student learning and teachers' practices are influenced by perceptions of teachers' collective efficacy. They formulated a conceptual model to explain the influence of collective efficacy in decision making related to student achievement. Their findings indicate "that perceived collective efficacy is a potent way to characterize school culture. Indeed, collective efficacy beliefs are more strongly related to teachers' perceptions of self-capability than many more common measures of school context" (p. 9).

Hoy, W. On his website at http://www.waynekhoy.com/#, Wayne Hoy has a number of research instruments concerning organizational climate, academic optimism, collective trust, collective efficacy, and many more topics.

Ladson-Billings, G. (1994). *The dreamkeepers: Successful teachers of African American children.* San Francisco, CA: Jossey-Bass. The author investigates good teaching that is culturally relevant. Specifically, she identifies longitudinal research associated with teachers who use successful practices with African American students who have been underserved by American schools. She illustrates the importance of getting students to strive for academic excellence in the classroom, no matter what their cultural identity.

References

Banks, J. A. (1999). Multicultural education in the new century. *The School Administrator, 56,* 8–10.

Barber, T. (1973). Pitfalls in research: nine investigator and experimenter effects. In R. M. W. Travers (Ed.), *Second handbook of research on teaching.* Chicago: Rand McNally.

Boykin, A. W., & Cunningham, R. T. (2001). The effects of movement expressiveness in story context and learning context on the analogical reasoning performance of African American children. *The Journal of Negro Education, 70*(1), 72–83.

Brookover, W. B., Beady, C., Flood, P., Schweitzer, J., & Wisenbaker, J. (1979). *School social systems and student achievement: Schools can make a difference.* New York: Praeger.

Brophy, J. E. (1983). Research on the self-fulfilling prophecy and teacher expectations. *Journal of Educational Psychology, 75*(5), 631–661. doi: 10.1037/0022–0663.75.5.631

Brophy, J. E., & Good, T. L. (1974). *Teacher–student relationships: Causes and consequences.* Holt, Rinehart & Winston: Oxford, England.

Brown, A. (1980). Research role of American Indian social scientists. *Journal of Educational Equity and Leadership, 1*(1), 47–59.

Cambron-McCabe, N., Cunningham, L. L., Harvey, J., & Koff, R. H. (2005). *The superintendent's fieldbook. A guide for leaders of learning.* Thousand Oaks, CA: Corwin.

Castagno, A. E., & Brayboy, B. M. J. (2008). Culturally responsive schooling for indigenous youth: A review of the literature. *Review of Educational Research, 78,* 941–993.

Cotton, K. (2003). *Principals and student achievement: What the research says.* Alexandria, VA: Association for Supervision and Curriculum Development.

Council of Chief State School Officers. (1996, November). *Interstate school leaders licensure consortium. Standards for school leaders.* Washington, DC: Author.

Deal, T., & Peterson, K. (1990). *The principal's role in changing school culture.* Washington, DC: U.S. Department of education, Office of Educational Research and Improvement.

Deyhle, D. (1992). Constructing failure and maintaining cultural identity: Navajo and Ute school leavers. *Journal of American Indian Education, 31*(2), 24–47.

Demmert, W. J., Jr. (2001). *Improving academic performance among Native American students: A review of the research literature.* Charleston, WV: ERIC Clearinghouse on Rural Education and Small Schools, Appalachian Educational Laboratory.

Diamond, J. B., Randolph, A., & Spillane, J. P. (2004). Teacher expectations and sense of responsibility for student learning: The importance of race, class and organizational habitus. *Anthropology & Education Quarterly, 35*(1), 75–98.

DiGiorgio, C. (2008). Negotiating cultural and academic expectations in a minority language school: The inclusive and exclusive effects of a principal's vision. *International Journal in Education, 11*(2), 169–189.

Dill, E. M., & Boykin, A. W. (2000). The comparative influence of individual, peer tutoring and communal learning contexts on the text recall of African American children. *Journal of Black Psychology, 26*, 65–78.

Edmonds, R. (1979). Effective schools for the urban poor. *Educational Leadership, 37*, 15–-24.

Farkas, G. (2003). Racial disparities and discrimination in education: What do we know, how do we know it, and what do we need to know? *Teachers College Press, 105*(6), 1119–1146.

Goddard, R. D. (2001). Collective efficacy: A neglected construct in the study of schools and student achievement. *Journal of Educational Psychology, 93*(3), 467–476.

Goddard, R. D., Hoy, W. K., & Hoy, A. W. (2000). Collective teacher efficacy: Its meaning, measure, and impact on student achievement. *American Educational Research Journal,37*(2), 479–507.

Goddard, R. D., Hoy, W. K., & Hoy, A. W. (2004). Collective efficacy beliefs, theoretical developments, empirical evidence, and future directions. *Educational Researcher, 33*(3), 3–13.

Goldenberg, C., Gallimore, R., Reese, L., & Garnier, H. (2001). Cause and effect? A longitudinal study of immigrant Latino parents' aspirations and expectations, and their children's school performance. *38* (3), 547–582.

Greenbaum, P., & Greenbaum, S. (1983). Cultural differences, nonverbal regulation, and classroom interaction: Sociolinguistic interference in American Indian education. *Peabody Journal of Education, 60*(4), 16–33.

Hallinger, P., & Heck, R. M. (1996). Reassessing the principal's role in school effectiveness: A review of empirical research, 1980–1995. *Educational Administration Quarterly, 32* (1–2), 5–44.

Hallinger, P., & Murphy, J. F. (1987). Assessing and developing principal instructional leadership. *Educational Leadership*, 54–61.

Hao, L., & Bonstead-Bruns, M. (1998). Parent–child differences in educational expectations and the academic achievement of immigrant and native students. *Sociology of Education, 71*, 175–198.

Heck, R. M. (1992). Principal's instructional leadership and school performance: Implications for policy development. *Educational Evaluation and Policy Analysis, 14*(1), 21–34.

Hess, G. A. (1999). Expectations, opportunity, capacity, and will: The four essential components of Chicago school reform. *Educational Policy, 13*(4), 494–517.

Ladson-Billings, G. (1994). *The dreamkeepers: Successful teachers of African American children.* San Francisco, CA: Jossey-Bass.

Ladson-Billings, G. (1995a). But that's just good teaching: The case for culturally relevant pedagogy. *Theory into Practice, 34*(3), 159–165.

Ladson-Billings, G. (Fall 1995b). Toward a theory of culturally relevant pedagogy. *American Educational Research Association, 32*(3), 465–491.

Ladson-Billings, G. (1998). Teaching in dangerous times: Culturally relevant approaches to teacher assessment. *The Journal of Negro Education, 67*(3), 255–267.

Lee, V. E.,& Smith, J. B. (1996). Collective responsibility for learning and its effects on gains in achievement for early secondary school students. *American Journal of Education, 104*(2), 103–147.

Leithwood, K., & Jantzi, D. (1999). The relative effects of principal and teachers' sources of leadership on student engagement with school. *Educational Administration Quarterly, 35*, 679–706.

Lunenburg, F. C., & Ornstein, A. C. (2000). *Educational administration: Concepts and practices.* Belmont, CA: Wadsworth/Thompson Learning.

Manthey, G. (2006). Collective efficacy: Explaining school achievement. *Leadership, 35*(3), 23–24.

Marzano, R. J. (2003). *What works in schools: Translating research into action.* Association for Curriculum Development and Supervision.

McLaughlin, D. (1989). The sociolinguistics of Navajo literacy. *Anthropology and Education Quarterly, 20*(4), 275–290.

Ming, K., & Dukes, C. (2006, Fall). Fostering cultural competence through school-based routines. *Multicultural Education, 14*(1), 24–48.

Newmann, F. M., Rutter, R. A., & Smith, M. S. (1989). Organizational factors that affect school sense of efficacy, community, and expectations. *Sociology of Education, 62*, 221–238.

No Child Left Behind Act of 2001, 20 U.S.C. § 6301. (2002).

O'Donnell, R. J., & White, G. P. (2005). Within the accountability era: Principals' instructional leadership behaviors and student achievement. *NASSP Bulletin, 89*, 56–71.

Owings, W. A., Kaplan, L. S., & Nunnery, J. (2002). Principal quality ISLLC standards and student achievement: A Virginia study. *Journal of School Leadership, 15*(1), 99–119.

Pewewardy, C., & Hammer, P. C. (2003). *Culturally responsive teaching for American Indian students [ERIC Digest].*Charleston, WV: ERIC Clearinghouse on Rural Education and Small Schools.

Pinchot, G. (1996). Creating organizations with many leaders. In F. Hesselbein, M. Goldsmith, & R. Beckard (Eds.), *The leaders of the future* (pp.25–39). San Francisco, CA: Jossey-Bass.

Pounder, D. G., Ogawa, R. T., & Adams, E. A. (1995). Leadership as an organization-wide phenomenon: Its impact on school performance. *Educational Administration Quarterly, 31*(4), 564–588.

Proctor, P. C. (1984). Teacher expectations: A model for school improvement. *The Elementary School Journal, 84*(4), 469–481.

Rist, R. C. (2000). HER classic: Student social class and teacher expectations: The self-fulfilling prophecy in ghetto education. *Harvard Educational Review, 70*(3), 257–302.

Rosenthal, R., & Jacobson, L. (1968). *Pygmalion in the classroom: Teacher expectation and pupils' intellectual development.* New York: Holt, Rinehart & Winston.

Schein, E. H. (1997). *Organizational culture and leadership,* 2nd ed. San Francisco, CA: Jossey-Bass.

Sergiovanni, T. J. (1999). Refocusing leadership to build community. *The High School Magazine, 7*(1), 11–15.

Sergiovanni, T. J., & Starratt, R. J. (1998). *Supervision: A redefinition,* 6th ed. Boston, MA: McGraw-Hill.

Snow, R. (1969). Unfinished Pygmalion. *Contemporary Psychology, 14,* 197–199.

Terry, R. W. (1993). *Authentic leadership: Courage in action.* San Francisco, CA: Jossey-Bass.

Thorndike, R. (1968). Review of *Pygmalion in the classroom* by Robert Rosenthal & Lenore Jacobson. *American Educational Research Journal, 5,* 708–711.

Ubben, G. C., & Hughes, L. W. (1997). *The principal: Creative leadership for schools,* 3rd ed. Needham Heights, MA: Allyn-Bacon.

Waters, J. T., Marzano, R. J., & McNulty, B. (2004). Leadership that sparks learning. *Educational Leadership, 61*(7), 48–51.

Weinstein, R. S., Madison, S. M., & Kuklinski, M. R. (1995). Raising expectations in schooling: Obstacles and opportunities for change. *American Educational Research Journal, 32*(1), 121–159.

Witziers, B., Bosker, R. J., & Kruger, M. L. (2003). Educational leadership and student achievement: The elusive search for an association. *Educational Administration Quarterly, 39,* 398–425.

5

Distributive and Empowering Leadership

LOUANN BIERLEIN PALMER

Similar to other areas of school reform, the concepts of *distributive and empowering leadership* within the school building have been proposed and studied for the past several decades. This chapter will summarize what these concepts mean (and the many terms associated with them), why the focus on these ideas, what research has revealed, and advice for practitioners working on improvements in their schools.

What Is Distributive and Empowering Leadership?

The concept of *sharing leadership* (or sharing the power of influence which comes with leadership) is not new. During the late 1980s and early 1990s, the concept of school-based decision-making was in vogue, whereby schools (not the district central office) needed to be greater hubs of power. Those closest to the implementation of a given decision would be allowed to make major decisions, and greater empowerment (and quality) would occur. Also during this time, the concept of teacher career levels (e.g., master teachers, career ladders) was tried as a way to include teachers in shared decision making and to incentivize individual teachers. Mixed results with such school-based decision-making occurred as principals struggled to take control of some budgetary issues, and to involve teachers (and parents) in meaningful ways. There were also concerns that the enhanced teacher roles/career levels directed teachers' energy toward managerial tasks rather than instructional support, and focused on individual job enhancement rather than collective community (Mangin & Stoelinga, 2008).

By the mid-to late-1990s the term *teacher leader* had emerged and often became associated with those who left the classroom to work in various instructional support positions (e.g., curriculum developer, teacher mentor). Many such positions were (and still are) supported by various federal programs (e.g., Reading First), and the No Child Left Behind Act of 2001's enhanced focus on instructional improvement also served to formalize many such positions. The belief is that such "instructional teacher leadership roles can facilitate instructional development—sustained, supported, and school-embedded opportunities to learn about the core technologies of teaching" (Mangin & Stoelinga, 2008, p. 3). Indeed, meta-analysis work by York-Barr and Duke (2004) found the concept and practice of teacher leadership had gained momentum, and that teachers were assuming more leadership functions at both instructional and organizational levels. Overall the emphasis was on teachers playing a key role in improving school practices and overall outcomes (Manno & Firestone, 2008).

During the mid-2000s continued focus on various aspects of shared leadership (beyond teacher leadership) were also occurring. Spillane (2006) is often associated with the early use of the word distributive leadership. He identified three arrangements for distributing leadership responsibilities: division of labor (different leaders for different tasks), co-performance (multiple leaders together for same task), and parallel performance (multiple leaders perform the same tasks but in different contexts). While all involve some distribution of power, Spillane notes distributive leadership is not necessarily the "act" of distributing power but the mindset (or perspective) a given leader takes about how to operate within a given organization (like a school). It involves capturing the role formal and informal leadership can (and should) play within an organization. Distributive leadership is also very contextual, with different patterns of power sharing needed depending on the situation at hand (Spillane & Diamond, 2007).

As we now find ourselves in the second decade of this century, distributive leadership often describes school leader actions taken to empower teachers to fully engage in school renewal. Spillane (2006) acknowledges that distributive leadership has become a catchall term and often a synonym for things like *democratic leadership, shared leadership, collaborative leadership, empowering leadership*, and *co-leadership*. Such term ambiguity causes grief for researchers on their journey to better understand the nuances of the issues. For practitioners, however, exact definitional clarity is not essential to actually implement some best practices, including the fostering of teacher leadership as an essential aspect of distributive leadership (Lieberman & Miller, 2004). Therefore much of this chapter will focus on using distributive and empowering leadership to identify, promote, and sustain teacher leaders. But first, let us review some core research findings on these topics.

Research on Distributive and Empowering Leadership

During the past decade significant research has revealed correlates associated with student outcomes, and the role of leadership. In their groundbreaking meta-analysis, Marzano, Waters, and McNulty (2005) identified 21 building-level leadership responsibilities or behaviors and calculated an average correlation between each and student learning. Indeed, later work by Marzano and Waters (2009) found that district-level leadership is also linked to student outcomes, and its greatest impact was associated with simultaneous "loose-tight" leadership strategies, allowing schools and teachers discretion in some areas while having controls on the classroom and administrative matters with the greatest impact on student learning. Similar work by other researchers (e.g., Leithwood, Mascall, & Strauss, 2009; Reeves, 2006) has clearly found that leadership and the appropriate "sharing" or distributing of power associated with leadership makes a difference.

Although many leadership studies use case studies or other qualitative methods to assess the impact of shared leadership, empirically based evidence also exists. For example, a recent four-year longitudinal study in 195 elementary schools found "significant direct effects of distributed leadership on change in the schools' academic capacity and indirect effects on students' growth rates in math" (Heck & Hallinger, 2009, p. 659). Supplementing this work with case studies of 21 schools that demonstrated high levels of reading growth, Hallinger and Heck (2010) conclude that leadership acts as "driver" in building a school's academic capacity and explicitly links a more team-oriented and collaborative approach to school leadership with increased capacity building strategies designed to impact teaching and learning.

Another recent groundbreaking research project was a six-year study of successful educational leadership practices, involving dozens of researchers and hundreds of school leaders across the country as funded by the Wallace Foundation (Louis, Leithwood, Wahlstrom, & Anderson, 2010). Given the comprehensive nature of this recent work, their major results related to distributive and empowering leadership will be summarized in this chapter.

First, let us review core findings from the portion of this research project examining the impact of *collective leadership*, the influence organizational members and stakeholders have on decisions in their schools. Key findings include:

- Collective leadership has a stronger influence on student achievement than individual leadership.
- Almost all people associated with high-performing schools have greater influence on school decisions than is the case with people in low-performing schools.
- Higher-performing schools award greater influence to teacher teams, parents, and students, in particular.
- Principals and district leaders have the most influence on decisions in all schools; however, they do not lose influence as others gain influence.
- Schools leaders have an impact on student achievement primarily through their influence on teachers' motivation and working conditions; their influence on teachers' knowledge and skills produces less impact on student achievement. (Louis et al., 2010, p. 19)

Within these findings, implications are that sharing power and influence with teachers is correlated to improved outcomes, and that such sharing does not reduce the influence of formal administrators. Also, shared leadership should focus on influencing teachers' motivation and workplace conditions as a means to impact student outcomes.

Another aspect of Louis et al.'s (2010) research project focused specifically on shared leadership (defined by them to denote teachers' influence over, and their participation in, school-wide decisions with principals), and its effect on classroom practice and student learning. They examined the effects of principals and teachers assuming shared responsibility for leadership and identified some conditions that influence this leadership approach. Core findings include:

- Leadership practices targeted directly at improving instruction have significant effects on teachers' working relationships and, indirectly, on student achievement.
- When principals and teachers share leadership, teachers' working relationships are stronger and student achievement is higher.
- Leadership effects on student achievement occur largely because effective leadership strengthens professional community—a special environment within which teachers work together to improve their practice and improve student learning. Professional community, in turn, is a strong predictor of

instructional practices that are strongly associated with student achievement.

- The link between professional community and student achievement may be explained by reference to a school climate that encourages levels of student effort above and beyond the levels encouraged in individual classrooms.
- The factor of trust is less significant than the factors of instructional leadership and shared leadership (although it is associated with both). (p. 37)

These findings reveal that shared leadership and instructional leadership are important variables, but they are only indirectly related to student achievement. Their power comes from helping to ensure certain teacher activities occur, including teachers organizing themselves into professional learning communities, reflective discussions about instruction, and a sense of collective responsibility for student learning. The authors concluded that shared leadership and instructional leadership are not "either/or" strategies but complementary approaches, and both may be necessary. They also note principals must:

> . . . take actions that support instructional and shared leadership which lead to improved student learning. Increasing teachers' involvement in the difficult task of making good decisions and introducing improved practices must be at the heart of school leadership. There is no simple short-cut. (p. 53)

A final aspect of Louis et al.'s (2010) extensive research project dealt with patterns of distributed leadership by principals. Core findings revealed:

- Although there are many sources of leadership in schools, principals remain the central source.
- How leadership is distributed in schools depends on what is to be accomplished, on the availability of professional expertise, and on principals' preferences regarding the use of professional expertise.
- No single pattern of leadership distribution is consistently linked to student learning.
- More complex and coordinated patterns of distributed leadership appear when school improvement initiatives focus directly on student learning goals as distinct from the implementation of specific programs. (p. 54)

A key take-away from these findings, especially since no single pattern of leadership distribution was linked to student learning, is that simply distributing leadership in a non-planned manner may be meaningless (having no real impact on student outcomes). Simply tossing out responsibilities and power to various teachers in a given school will probably mean little. The researchers also concluded there is currently no known best distribution pattern, since the tasks at hand, and the players involved, will depend on the circumstances.

Overall, Louis et al.'s (2010) research has provided additional empirical evidence linking shared leadership and *the creation of professional community* with improved student learning. The link is indirect in that principals impact teachers, who in turn impact student outcomes. Unfortunately, no recipe exists for the one best way to share (or distribute) the leadership power, but current evidence points to the creation of teacher leaders via professional learning communities, with such teachers engaged in practitioner-focused action research to determine what instructional strategies work best with their students. The next section details such best practices.

Best Practices for Distributing Leadership

As previously noted, creating teacher leaders is a key method of distributing leadership power within a school, with the goal of obtaining better student outcomes. Although there is no magic bullet for the identification and nurturing of teacher leaders, principals can strive to establish a culture of teacher leadership within their schools. Important practices include understanding the role of teacher leaders, developing professional learning communities, helping teachers to become active practitioner researchers, and overcoming known barriers to teacher leadership. Let us review each of these practices.

Understanding the Role of Teacher Leaders

Before we can create something, we first need to better understand the concept. To this end, Katzenmeyer and Moller (2009) offer four characteristics of teacher leaders, whereby such individuals: (1) lead within and beyond the classroom; (2) contribute to a community of learners and leaders; (3) influence others toward improved practice; and (4) accept responsibility for outcomes. Mangin and Stoelinga (2008) describe today's teacher leaders as nonsupervisory, focused on instructional improvement and teachers' capacity building. Given these characteristics, it would be very desirable to have one or more individuals within a school exhibiting such characteristics.

Teacher leaders may be engaged in more "formal" positions (e.g., instructional coach, mentor, department chair), which some consider quasi-administrative positions because such teachers are no longer in their own classroom for some or all of their time. Increasingly, however, "informal" teacher leaders are being identified, nurtured, and valued by both their peers and administrators (Stoelinga, 2008). Such informal teacher leaders choose not to leave their classrooms but influence other teachers through casual conversations, sharing teaching materials, facilitating professional development, and other supportive activities. Indeed, current thinking on informal teacher leadership is that it should not be something separate from and added to teachers' classroom work, but that peer-to-peer leadership activities must become the basis of teachers' work (Smylie, 2008). Here are just a few of the many potential formal and informal leadership roles for teacher leaders:

- Assume a more comprehensive teacher's role, which includes becoming more knowledgeable about professional and research issues.
- Serve as instructional resource persons in the school and be available for peer coaching.
- Serve as mentors to beginning teachers. Assist them with course planning, classroom organization, delivery of instruction, and personal issues such as stress associated with entering the profession.
- As department or team leaders, recommend communication links, coordinate curriculum planning, and suggest staff development guidelines based on research findings.
- Provide the knowledge base for issues discussed in school improvement meetings.
- As members of local evaluation teams, investigate local school curriculum practices using standards and recent evaluation techniques.
- Assist with local dissemination of information about trends in curriculum research.
- Identify solutions for local problems that can lead to better schools.
- Organize action research groups and share results with other teachers and administrators. (Austin Independent School District, n.d.)

Is there really a group of teachers within each school willing to become teacher leaders? Those who have been working with schools on this concept for many years would answer a strong "yes" to this question, noting:

> Within every school there is a *sleeping giant* of teacher leadership that can be a catalyst for making changes to improve student learning. . . . By helping teachers recognize that they are leaders, by offering opportunities to develop their leadership skills, and by creating school cultures that honor their leadership, we can awak-

en this sleeping giant of teacher leadership. (Katzenmeyer & Moller, 2009, pp. 2–3)

Researchers have also found several benefits of having one or more teacher leaders in a school: enhanced professional efficacy and retention of excellent teachers, less resistance to change as teacher leaders positively influence other teachers, career enhancement and opportunities for self-improvement, enhanced accountability for results, and increased chances for sustainable reforms (Katzenmeyer & Moller, 2009; Lieberman & Miller, 2004; Mangin & Stoelinga, 2008). Because changes take time, teacher leaders can continue reform momentum when a given principal is transferred or otherwise leaves. Such teacher leaders not only carry on reforms but can provide transitional support to new leaders. Once again, these are very desirable outcomes for every school principal. The next section offers some details on how to achieve such teacher leadership outcomes.

Developing Professional Learning Communities

Researchers have found that teacher leaders often "are found" and/or are developed via professional learning committees (Lieberman & Friedrich, 2010; York-Barr & Duke, 2004). So cultivating an active learning community within a school will serve to also cultivate teacher leaders. Such professional learning communities require:

1. Supportive and shared leadership: School administrators participate democratically with teachers—sharing power, authority, and decision making.
2. Shared values and vision: School administrators and teachers share visions for school improvement that have an undeviating focus on student learning and that are consistently referenced for the staff's work.
3. Collective learning and application of learning: Faculty and staff collective learning and application of the learning (taking action) create high intellectual learning tasks and solutions to address student needs.
4. Supportive conditions: School conditions and human capacities support the staff's arrangement as a professional learning organization.
5. Shared personal practice. Peers review and give feedback on teacher instructional practice in order to increase individual and organizational capacity. (Hord, 2003, p. 7)

These are difficult pieces to obtain, yet many principals would currently indicate the existence of professional learning communities in their school. Indeed the term is now being used to describe nearly any collection or committee of teachers working together on any task (DuFour, 2004). Yet the heart of a professional learning community is when teachers are purposively organized into collaborative teams which focus their efforts on critically examining teaching and learning practices. The honest answers to several key questions will reveal whether a processional learning community exists within a given organization:

1. Do we use data to assess our individual and collective effectiveness? Do assessment results help us learn from one another in ways that positively affect our classroom practice?
2. Does our team work interdependently to achieve SMART goals that are Strategic (linked to school goals), Measurable, Attainable, Results-oriented (focused on evidence of student learning rather than teacher strategies), and Time-bound?
3. Are continuous improvement processes built into our routine work practices?
4. Do we make decisions by building shared knowledge regarding best practices rather than simply pooling opinions?
5. Do we use our collaborative team time to focus on these critical issues? (DuFour, 2007, p. 5)

Unfortunately, once principals consider this list of questions as a way to measure whether true professional learning committees exist in their schools, far fewer will lay claim to such entities. Yet, the research is now clear that teacher practices and the ongoing dialogue and critical examination of teaching and learning by all members within a school are essential. Indeed, because student achievement is firmly connected to adult behavior, building teacher leadership capacity is not a diversion but a necessity (Lambert, 2003).

So what role do principals play in creating such professional learning communities and teacher leaders? Research is clear that the role of the principal is not diminished once teacher leadership is embraced (Louis et al., 2010). The principal's role shifts to that of a "talent scout, constantly on the prowl for effective practice" (Reeves, 2008, p. 71). Principals should perform the following functions:

1. Build the confidence of teachers to be leaders. Make yourself available for regular interactions with perspective teacher leaders, and authentically listen to their ideas.
2. Support teachers in initiatives they wish to lead and remove barriers to their success.

3. Find ways to give incentives (e.g., release time, resources, recognition, and problem-solving assistance) to teachers who are willing to take on leadership. (Katzenmeyer & Moller, 2009, pp. 21–22)

Overall, the role of the principal is to develop professional learning communities, which will help them find and nurture teacher leaders, who, in turn, can help to nurture other teachers.

Helping Teacher Leaders Become Active "Researchers"

Reeves (2006, 2008, 2010) is an active researcher on school reform efforts and has contributed much to the knowledge base. One of his core findings is that deep implementation is needed for any instructional practice to really make a difference on student achievement. His research has found significant differences in outcomes depending on the percentage of teachers implementing a given strategy. For example, a school in which only 10% of the teachers consistently implemented the classroom strategy of "writing and note taking" in science only had 25% of their students on a "proficient" level. This is compared to a school in which 90% of teachers were implementing that strategy, resulting in a 79% student proficiency rate. While Reeves (2008) admits such data involve correlations, not causations, they do demonstrate clearly that "deep implementation at the 90% level of teaching practice is associated with strikingly higher levels of student achievement" (p. 16). Given his research and the work of many others (e.g., Marzano et al., 2005), Reeves now argues that the question is no longer whether teaching and leadership matter but how we best expand and extend the most powerful teaching and leadership strategies.

Reeves' (2008) findings have led to the conclusion that teachers observing and coaching teachers must become the new foundation of professional development, and he advocates the need to engage teachers in *action research projects* on a sustained basis in a collaborative environment. His research has found that "teacher researchers affect the professional practices of their colleagues" (p. 8) and that "effective professional practices are reinforced and repeated not only by the original teacher researchers but also by many other teachers who are influenced by these observations and practices" (p. 8). The implications are that teachers need to critically examine aspects of their practice and collect data on efforts to improve such practices. Such practices can only occur once teachers are immersed within professional learning communities and a level of trust has been created (Reeves, 2010).

After working with teacher leaders for many years, Katzenmeyer and Moller (2009) also advocate that action research "engages teacher leaders in disciplined inquiry conducted to inform and improve practice by using the results and other research" (p. 56). They have found such activities serve as a powerful form of continuous professional learning for experienced teacher leaders. Teacher leaders develop an *Influencing Action Plan* in which they identify a problem for which they might be able to impact the situation, look for possible solutions and best practices from other schools, and then take some actions to help solve the problem. They note that "action research is a growing phenomenon, as teacher leaders realize that they can use their learning not only to impact their own situations but also to influence others towards improved practice" (Katzenmeyer & Moller, 2009, p. 115). Sample action projects from teacher leaders they worked with include teacher collaboration to integrate social studies into art lessons; the establishment of the first multiage classroom in an elementary school; the moving of high school-aged, trainable mentally disabled students from a middle school classroom to the high school; and the formation of consistent discipline procedures for students when they are in special classes. Although such projects may appear to be simple reform activities, the difference is that data (as collected by teachers) were used to make decisions throughout the process.

Thornton (2010) has also found that action research can be used by teachers to study what is happening within their schools and then to find solutions to learning barriers. She worked with teachers who used action research projects to examine teacher leadership, identifying the status of such leadership in their schools as well as barriers. Action plans were developed to address the primary barriers, including a timeline for implementation and identified key participants. Solutions they found and worked to implement included having teacher leaders periodically plan and run staff meetings focused on sharing best practices, problem solving, and offering teachers a vehicle for voice and change; and reallocating professional development funds to teacher leaders in the building to facilitate PD sessions (instead of outside speakers or consultants). Lieberman and Friedrich (2010) also found that teachers "through asking questions, collecting and analyzing data, and talking with peers, these teachers . . . feel empowered to questions mandates and be part of change" (p. 31). Such teachers become leaders working to creating opportunities and communities that challenge the status quo.

Finally, although the term "research" sounds scary and only doable by those at the higher education level, *action* research (or *practitioner* research as recoined by Cochran-Smith & Lytle, 2009), takes place when teachers are observing their own students and their own professional practices. It is messy, non-perfect work, but the "reward of local credibility and teachers' influence on one another is enormous" (Reeves, 2008, p. 35). It involves teachers themselves critically examining their teaching practices, and initially collecting information (i.e., data) on some first-order changes to see what happens, and then as confidence builds, on some second order changes that break with the past (Marzano et al., 2005). It has principals encouraging and empowering their teachers to improve practice in their own classrooms and then sharing that information with their peers as teacher leaders.

Overcoming Barriers to Teachers Becoming Leaders

As with any significant change, there are always barriers to implementation. Researchers have identified several, which, if understood upfront by principals, might be mitigated.

Teachers often feel they do not have the knowledge and skills to lead other adults. Their formal university programs, both at the undergraduate and graduate level, rarely include leadership-based courses nor does the professional development they receive. The trick is to help teachers realize that the tools they use to successfully teach students are the same tools that can be used to work with (and "lead") adults. Leading, like teaching, involves facilitating the acquisition and implementation of new knowledge.

More difficult barriers to overcome are the egalitarian norms of school cultures, which may discourage teachers from drawing attention to themselves (Katzenmeyer & Moller, 2009). This has been driven by the flat structure within most schools, and the traditional salary structures paying the same based on years of experience and education levels. Research has found that teachers who step into formal leadership positions may "risk rejection, isolation, and resistance from former peers" (Lieberman & Friedrich, 2010, p. 7). Collegial jealousy exists from those not selected to serve in teacher leadership positions (Thornton, 2010). Fortunately this culture of "sameness" is changing as teachers are more readily embracing leadership from their peers.

Related to both the lack of confidence to work with adults and the egalitarian school norms, is the strong "teacher identity" that successful teachers have created. In examining closely "how" teachers become leaders, Lieberman and Friedrich (2010) found the need for such teacher leaders to create a new identify. Because many teacher leaders leave the classroom for some or all of their day but do not become formal administrators, they suddenly find themselves not fitting in either world. Principals need to be aware of this identify concern and allow time and support for such identify adjustments.

Another barrier is the real extent to which teachers are being offered opportunities to become leaders, which is driven in large part by how comfortable the principal is with sharing power. Thornton (2010) found that principals who are authoritative preferred to make decisions alone, and teacher leadership in those schools was often relegated to committees where teachers felt they were only implementing predetermined plans. On the other hand, she found that when principals were too laissez-faire and offered little presence, there was limited teacher buy-in and conflicts among teachers trying to take charge of a situation. Louis et al. (2010) concluded that the profession has become enamored of distributed forms of leadership, but principals must really want such a culture within their schools if it is to work.

Putting It into Practice—An Interview with Two Teachers

Empowering and distributive leadership requires the creation of a healthy school culture in which adequate leadership capacity can be developed and teacher leaders can thrive. Of course, this is much easier said than done. The following interview, "comparing and contrasting" two beginning teachers in different schools (as taken from Katzenmeyer & Moller, 2009), helps to bring these concepts to life.

How would you describe the professional development and learning for new teachers like yourself?

Sarah: I would say we have a pseudo-mentoring program; you know, my mentor is a great person, and she says if you need any help come and see me, but there is no structure, no released time for us to get together, and no specific expectations. So far, I have not participated in any formal professional development activities this semester except the pre-school day for new teachers.

Anthony: I like that my principal is always sharing articles and books with us; he leads a study group that we can attend on Tuesday mornings if we are interested in discussing the readings with other teachers. I am impressed that the principal frequently stops in and has offered for me to visit some colleagues' classrooms. My mentor is working with me on the new curriculum we are implement and has already modeled several lessons with my students while I observed him.

How are you encouraged to make improvements or to be innovative?

Sarah: I am told that resources at my school are pretty limited due to budget cutbacks. I don't have my own classroom yet, so I find it hard to experiment and be creative. . . . My department head is happy that my classes are an improvement over the situation last year, when the students had a full time substitute who was not certified in science.

Anthony: I have the support of the literacy coach to help me implement the strategies for reading in the content area, and she is encouraging me to adapt or adjust them for my particular students. She observes my lessons and coaches me on how to improve them as we discuss my own ideas about how the lesson worked. The assistant principal has offered her help if I want to continue to move toward more differentiation in instruction. She say she will help by reviewing my plans ahead of time and coteaching my classes as I learn to manage multiple groups of students working on different levels. We are also using a process called "classroom walkthrough" that involves colleagues walking through our classes and then meeting with us to discuss their observations. I am looking forward to hearing their insights, and I hope to do walkthrough myself next year. It's a lot to learn, but I think all of these initiatives can make a difference with my students.

How do you collaborate on instructional or student-related matters?

Sarah: I can talk to my mentor and if I need them, I think my administrators would be willing to meet with me. Most of the experienced teachers had been here a long time and seem to keep to themselves pretty much. I feel like a new kid on the block.

Anthony: I have already mentioned the literacy coach, the principal, the assistant principal, and my other department members, with whom I interact frequently. Faculty meetings are structured so we work with other teachers outside our own teams and departments. I recently worked with one of our special education teachers on identifying some strategies to work with a struggling student. I feel like there are many opportunities to discuss, share, and learn with my colleagues in this school. (Katzenmeyer & Moller, 2009, pp. 86–89)

Although these "interviews" involved beginning teachers, one can clearly see differences within the culture of their schools. Anthony is lucky enough to be working in a school where teacher leadership practices are evident. He is receiving formal and informal mentoring, there is on-going learning via study groups, and there is trust in approaching his principal about issues. The more experienced teachers in his school are engaged in self-reflection and the early stages of practitioner research. The principal relies upon such teacher leaders to help Anthony focus on the core aspects of teaching and learning.

Sarah, unfortunately, has none of these things. And research indicates that the distributive leadership practices within Anthony's school will lead to improved student outcomes, while those in Sarah's school will not. The following section offers some valuable resources to help support the creation of a school culture similar to Anthony's school.

Resources to Help Assess Your School and Teachers for Leadership

The evidence is clear that teacher behaviors do impact student outcomes and that the creation of real professional learning communities and teacher leaders enhances such behaviors. If you are ready to take on this challenge, an initial step is to assess the current status of your school and teachers. Several researchers have created tools to assist in that effort.

Teacher Leadership Readiness Assessment Surveys

Katzenmeyer and Moller (2009) include several assessment tools of value. The first is *Assessing Your Readiness for Teacher Leadership*, a simple self-assessment tool for teachers to reflect upon their own personal beliefs and strengths regarding their potential role as a formal or informal teacher leader. For those teachers who are already engaged in leadership activities, there is a *Teacher Leadership Self-Assessment*, which allows reflection on how well they are fulfilling that role, and what areas they may wish to seek additional professional development. Lastly, these authors have developed the *Teacher Leadership School Survey*, a tool for principals to gather information from all teachers in a school regarding the extent to which a culture of active teacher leadership is occurring within a given building.

The Center for Strengthening the Teaching Profession, an independent non-profit organization located in Tacoma, Washington, also offers several assessment tools (available at no cost on-line). Teacher leaders can use the Teacher Leadership Self-Assessment to assess their current knowledge and skills and plan for their future development as leaders. School principals and other school and district leaders can use the School and District Capacity Tool to determine systems-level readiness to utilize the expertise of teacher leaders and support their work and development as leaders.

Leadership Capacity Assessment and Transition Frameworks

Lambert's (2003, 2006) research has revealed a framework assessing the *leadership capacity* of a given school, the broad-based, skillful participation of teachers in the work of leadership, including their understanding of sustainable school improvement. Figure 5.1 offers a picture of four possible stages for school environments: quadrant 1 involves low skillfulness and low teacher leadership participation levels, and quadrant 4 involves high levels of both skillfulness and teacher leadership participation. Lambert notes that complex issues do not divide neatly into boxes, and schools may find themselves in more than one box.

All principals would want their schools to be classified in quadrant 4. Yet a recent study by Thornton (2010) found that even after implementing significant reforms, 59% of schools studied were barely within quadrant 3 due to their limited use of schoolwide data, polarized staff, scattered pockets of excellence and innovation, and relatively static student achievement.

Quadrant 1	**Quadrant 2**
• Principal as autocratic manager • Limited (one-way) flow of information; no shared visions • Codependent, paternal/maternal relationships; rigidly defined roles • Norms of compliance; blame; program coherence technical and superficial • Lack of innovation in teaching and learning • Student achievement is poor, or showing short-term improvements on standardized measures	• Principal as "laissez-faire" manager; many teachers developing unrelated programs • Fragmentation and lack of coherence of information, and programs' lack of shared purpose • Norms of individualism, lack of collective responsibility • Undefined roles and responsibilities • Spotty innovation with both excellent and poor classrooms • Student achievement appears static overall (unless data are disaggregated)
Quadrant 3	**Quadrant 4**
• Principal and key teachers as purposeful leadership team • Limited uses of school-wide data, information flow within designated leadership groups • Polarized staff, pockets of strong resistance • Strong reflection, innovation, and teaching excellence among selected teachers; program coherence still weak • Student achievement static or showing slight improvement	• Principal and teachers, as well as parents and students, are skillful learners • Shared vision results in program coherence • Inquiry-based use of information to inform decision and practices • Roles and actions reflect broad involvement, collaboration, and collective responsibility • Reflective practice consistently leads to innovation • Student achievement is high or improving steadily

Figure 5.1 Leadership Capacity of Four School Types Source: Adapted from Lambert, 2006, p. 240). Reprinted by permission of the publisher (Taylor & Francis Ltd., http://www.tandf.co.uk/journals, #2932250306825).

Lambert's (2006) research also studied schools as they moved toward quadrant 4 and captured the phases they encountered as they progressed to the highest level. Figure 5.2 summarizes the principal's role, as he or she moves from being a "teacher, sponsor, and director" in the initial instructive phrase, to being a "colleague, critical friend, and mentor" in the high leadership capacity phase.

The initial *instructive phase* involves establishing collaborative structures and processes (e.g., teams, a school vision, examination of data, shared expectations, and processes for working together). It is also a time when teachers need the principal to provide support so that relationships and identities can begin to shift into new patterns. There is also resistance, disengagement, and continued dependence on the principal to make key decisions.

Instructive Phase	Transitional Phase	High Leadership Capacity Phase
Principal as teacher, sponsor, director	***Principal as guide, coach***	***Principal as colleague, critical friend, mentor***
Personal attributes and behaviors • Learns continually • Thinks strategically • Value/vision driven • Sets norms with staff • Supervises/ensures staff accountability • Convenes conversations • Honors history • Sponsors staff growth • Accepts responsibility • Breaks dependencies • Clarifies roles	Personal attributes and behaviors • Learns—attends to epiphanies • Thinks strategically • Translates values into vision language • Lets go, provides support, and sticks around • Scaffolds with ideas and questions • Mediates roles • Develops structures that build reciprocal relationships • Coaches for instructional improvement	Personal attributes and behaviors • Learns continually • Thinks strategically • Value/vision driven • Continues and expands behaviors initiated in earlier phases
• Articulates strategies • Creates safe, "holding" environment		
Instructs staff (or arranges for instruction) in: • Collaboration, group processes, and teaming; • Conversation and dialogue; • Inquiry/data use; • Trust building; • Best instructional practices; • Communication skills • Facilitation; • Conflict resolution; and • Accountability	Guides staff to: • Develop shared vision; • Establish process observation or norms; • Use inquiry; • Question assumptions; • Conduct constructivist conversations; • Identify and solve problems; • Surface/mediate conflict; • Find resources (time, professional development, monies); and • Plan	Participates with other members of the community to: • Think strategically; • Share concerns/issues; • Share decisions; • Monitor and implement shared visions; • Engage in reflective practices (reflection/inquiry/dialogue/action); • Monitor norms and take-self corrective actions; • Build a culture of interdependency; • Self-organize; • Diversify and blend roles; • Establish criteria for self-accountability; • Share authority and responsibility (dependent on expertise and interest, rather than role); and • Plan for enculturation of new staff and succession
Uses formal authority to convene and maintain conversations, challenge complacency or incompetence, and make certain decisions	Uses formal authority to sustain conversations, insist on professional development and inquiry agenda, mediate the demands of the district and state, and set reform pace	Uses formal authority to implement community decisions, mediate political pressures, work with less than competent staff, and work on legal and reform challenges

Figure 5.2 Principal's Behaviors in Leadership Capacity Development (adapted from Lambert, 2006, p. 245). Reprinted by permission of the publisher (Taylor & Francis Ltd., http://www.tandf.co.uk/journals, #2932250306825).

The *transitional phase* involves letting go of power while still offering support and coaching. Principals must read when to pull back as teachers emerge into leaders, because such emergence occurs at varying rates (and for some teachers not at all). One principal knew she had arrived when "People don't line up to ask me questions. They ask one another" (Lambert, 2006, p. 248). A culture is created where teachers no longer need to ask the principal's permission and expect the principal to make the decisions and take care of them.

Within the last phrase—high leadership capacity—Lambert (2006) found the teachers' influence and actions begin to converge with the principals. Levels of reciprocity occur, as teacher leaders find their voice, and now they facilitate the conversations, frame the problems, or challenge assumptions. Is this possible? Lambert (2006) offers this example:

> Kelly Elementary School is an example of a school that moved through the three growth phases. When the principal was hired, the school was the lowest performing school in the city and was under threat of closure. During her three-year tenure, the principal built trusting relationships by tearing down the boundaries among personal and professional roles. Retreats were held on a houseboat. Student learning became the focus. New teachers were hired and mentored into the new environment. The principal assumed a strong lead initially but then encouraged strong collaboration. Two staff members overcame their initial resistance and began to participate when they were convinced that student achievement was improving . . . when a new principal was hired, the teachers became concerned that they were losing momentum and asked their external coach for assistance. Today, with a new half-time principal, the school is a high leadership capacity school. (p. 250)

The information within Figure 5.2 can be used by principals as a guide for their own behavior as they create professional learning communities within their schools, cultivating and nurturing teacher leaders

Annotated Bibliographies for Suggested Reading

There are many book and articles available on creating professional learning communities and teacher leaders and several books and websites noted below.

Katzenmeyer, M., & Moller, G. (2009). *Awakening the sleeping giant: Helping teachers develop as leaders* (3rd ed.). Thousand Oaks, CA: Corwin. This book offers complete teacher leadership and school assessment tools (as described in this chapter) in its appendix.

Reeves, D. B. (2008). *Reframing teacher leadership to improve your school.* Alexandria, VA: Association for Supervision and Curriculum Development. This book describes how professional learning communities and teacher leader action research can be used to promote effective change.

Materials from the Center for Strengthening the Teaching Profession (CSTP) can be found at http://www.cstp-wa.org/teacher-development/teacher-leadership/skills-framework. Their framework articulates the specific knowledge and skills needed to be an effective teacher leader and offers free teacher leader and school/district capacity assessment tools (as described in this chapter) on this website.

Teacher Leaders Network, A National Initiative of the Center for Teacher Quality, based in North Carolina, and available at teacherleaders.org. Their website offers a virtual gathering place for those interested in the advancement of teacher leadership.

Conclusion

This chapter has attempted to summarize current knowledge about distributing leadership via the practice of creating teacher leaders. It has highlighted current research that empirically links such leadership practices to improved student outcomes via its impact on teacher behaviors. Unfortunately, there is still no prescribed method for creating a culture of teacher leadership within a school (and there probably never will be given the "art" of teaching and learning), but certain best practices do exist including understanding the role of teacher leaders, developing professional learning communities, helping teachers to become active practitioner researchers, and overcoming known barriers to teacher leadership. It all starts with assessing the current leadership capacity of your school and teachers using several tools and frameworks provided, and remembering that:

> Teacher leadership offers exceptional promise for student achievement and faculty morale. Overcoming the barriers of blame, bureaucracy, and baloney is challenging, but the results are compelling. When we replace blame with efficacy, supplant bureaucracy with networks, and give evidence power over baloney, we open the doors. . . . (Reeves, 2008, p. 69)

References

Austin Independent School District, Office of Educator Quality—Teacher Leadership Development Program. (n.d.). Retrieved from http://archive.austinisd.org/teachers/teacher_leadership/index.phtml

Cochran-Smith, M., & Lytle, S. L. (2009). *Inquiry as stance: Practitioner research in the next generation.* New York: Teachers College Press.

DuFour, R. (2004). What is a professional learning community? *Educational Leadership, 61*(8), 6–11.

DuFour, R. (2007). Professional learning communities: A bandwagon, an idea worth considering, or our best hope for high levels of learning? *Middle School Journal, 39*(1), 4–8.

Hallinger, P., & Heck, R. H. (2010). Leadership for learning: Does collaborative leadership make a difference in school improvement? *Educational Management Administration & Leadership, 38,* 654–678.

Heck, R. H., & Hallinger, P. (2009). Assessing the contribution of distributed leadership to school improvement and growth in math achievement. *American Educational Research Journal, 46,* 659–689.

Hord, S. (2003). Introduction. In S. Hord (Ed.), *Learning together, leading together: Changing schools through professional learning communities* (pp. 1–14). New York: Teachers College Press.

Katzenmeyer, M., & Moller, G. (2009). *Awakening the sleeping giant: Helping teachers develop as leaders* (3rd ed.). Thousand Oaks, CA: Corwin.

Lambert, L. (2003). *Leadership capacity for lasting school improvement.* Alexandria, VA: Association for Supervision and Curriculum Development.

Lambert, L. (2006). Lasting leadership: A study of high leadership capacity schools. *The Educational Forum, 70*(3), 238–254.

Leithwood, K., Mascall, B., & Strauss, T. (Eds.). (2009). *Distributed leadership according to the evidence.* New York: Routledge.

Lieberman, A., & Friedrich, L. D. (2010). *How teachers become leaders: Leading from practice and research.* New York: Teachers College Press.

Lieberman, A., & Miller, L. (2004). *Teacher leadership.* San Francisco, CA: Jossey-Bass.

Louis, K. S., Leithwood, K., Wahlstrom, K. L., & Anderson, S. E. (2010). *Learning from leadership: Investigating the links to improved student learning.* St. Paul, MN: University of Minnesota, Center for Applied Research and Educational Improvement.

Mangin, M. M., & Stoelinga, S. R. (2008). Teacher leadership: What it is and why it matters. In M. M. Mangin & S. R. Stoelinga (Eds.), *Effective teacher leadership: Using research to inform and reform* (pp. 1–35). New York: Teachers College Press.

Manno, C. M., & Firestone, W. A. (2008). Content is the subject: How teacher leaders with different subject knowledge interact with teachers. In M. M. Mangin & S. R. Stoelinga (Eds.), *Effective teacher leadership: Using research to inform and reform* (pp. 36–54). New York: Teachers College Press.

Marzano, R. J., & Waters, T. W. (2009). *District leadership that works: Striking the right balance.* Bloomington, IN: Solution Tree.

Marzano, R. J., Waters, T. W., & McNulty, B. A. (2005). *School leadership that works: From research to results.* Alexandria, VA: Association for Supervision and Curriculum Development.

Reeves, D. B. (2006). *The learning leaders: How to focus school improvement for better results.* Alexandria, VA: Association for Supervision and Curriculum Development.

Reeves, D. B. (2008). *Reframing teacher leadership to improve your school.* Alexandria, VA: Association for Supervision and Curriculum Development.

Reeves, D. B. (2010). *Transforming professional development into student results.* Alexandria, VA: Association for Supervision and Curriculum Development.

Smylie, M. A. (2008). Foreword. In M. M. Mangin & S. R. Stoelinga (Eds.), *Effective teacher leadership: Using research to inform and reform* (pp. ix–x). New York: Teachers College Press.

Spillane, J. P. (2006). *Distributed leadership.* San Francisco, CA: Jossey-Bass.

Spillane, J. P., & Diamond, J. B. (2007). *Distributed leadership in practice.* New York: Teachers College Press.

Stoelinga, S. R. (2008). Leading from above and below: Formal and informal teacher leadership. In M. M. Mangin & S. R. Stoelinga (Eds.), *Effective teacher leadership: Using research to inform and reform* (pp. 99–119). New York: Teachers College Press.

Thornton, H. J. (2010). Excellent teachers leading the way: How to cultivate teacher leadership. *Middle School Journal, 3*(6), 43.

York-Barr, J., & Duke, K. (2004). What do we know about teacher leadership? Findings from two decades of scholarship. *Review of Educational Research, 74*, 255–316.

6 Coherent Curriculum

JIANGANG XIA, JIANPING SHEN,
AND VAN E. COOLEY

Reform efforts may fail to improve student achievement if they fail to strengthen instructional program coherence within schools.
—Newmann, Smith, Allensworth, & Bryk, 2001b

What Is a Coherent Curriculum? An Introduction

In the literature, there are two major elements in a coherent curriculum. One element is the notion of horizontal and vertical articulation within the curriculum and the other moves beyond the first element to include alignment among standards, curriculum, learning experience, assessment, etc. In this chapter, we review the literature that reflects these two elements.

Horizontal and Vertical Articulation within the Curriculum

Beane (1995) introduced the metaphor of a jigsaw puzzle to guide us to understand the image of a coherent curriculum: when we work on a jigsaw puzzle, we usually need a picture of what the completed puzzle will look like, and none of the separate pieces means much until they begin to fit together. Beane has reminded us that this jigsaw puzzle metaphor depicts the way our students experience the curriculum in all too many schools:

> They move from one classroom to another, from one time block to another, from one textbook to another, from one teacher to another, confronted by disconnected, fragmented pieces of information or skills. For these young people, the curriculum is a pile of jigsaw puzzle pieces without a picture. (p. 1)

Beane (1995) believed this jigsaw puzzle metaphor should have some implications for educators. He edited the Association for Supervision and Curriculum Development (ASCD) 1995 yearbook *Toward a Coherent Curriculum,* in which he defined a coherent curriculum as "one that holds together, that makes sense as a whole; and its parts, whatever they are, are unified and connected by that sense of the whole" (p. 3). Beane believed that "a coherent curriculum has a sense of the forest as well as the trees, a sense of unity and connectedness, of relevance and pertinence" (p. 3).

The Center for Curriculum Materials in Science (CCMS) (see Roseman, Linn, & Koppal, 2008, pp. 16–17) shares a similar understanding of curricular coherence, arguing that the content of curriculum materials is coherent when it emphases a set of "interrelated ideas" and various "connections"—connections between the ideas of science and phenomena in the natural world, connections to prerequisite and other related ideas, and connections to evidence supporting the ideas. CCMS researchers have used these characteristics of coherent content as principles for curriculum development and as criteria for evaluating the content of existing curriculum materials (please see the Resource section of this chapter for more details).

Over time, the notion of horizontal and vertical articulation was also discussed by Johnson (1989), Silverman and Ennis (1996), and, more recently Schmidt, Houang, and Cougan (2002). With the advent of the standards movement, Schmidt et al. included "standards" as part of the concept of "horizontal and vertical articulation" and provided a definition of coherence in terms of both content standards and curricula:

> We define content standards and curricula to be coherent if they are articulated over time as a sequence of topics and performances that are logical and reflect, where appropriate, the sequential or hierarchical nature of the disciplinary content from which the subject matter derives. That is, what and how students are taught should reflect not only the topics that fall within a certain academic discipline, but also the key ideas that determine how knowledge is organized and generated within that discipline. (p. 9)

Schmidt et al. believed that "to be coherent" means content standards must evolve from particulars to deeper structures which connect the particulars. They argued the evolution from particulars to deeper structures should occur over the school year within a particular grade level and across grade levels as well. Schmidt and his colleagues (2002, 2005) believed coherence is one of the most important characteristics defining quality in content standards. They argued coherence itself implies the necessity, at least at some level, of uniformity across schools or districts.

Aligning Curriculum, Instruction, Assessment, and Others

Newmann, Smith, Allensworth, and Bryk (2001b) moved beyond the notion of "horizontal and vertical articulation" and proposed the notion of "instructional program coherence" which was defined as "a set of interrelated programs for students and staff that are guided by a common framework for curriculum, instruction, assessment, and learning climate and are pursued over a sustained period" (pp. 297, 299). They noticed coherent curriculum required for "sensible connections and coordination between the topics that students study in each subject within a grade and as they advance through the grades"(p. 298). They claimed instructional program coherence entails curricular coherence, conceptualizing instructional program coherence as an antecedent concept of curricular coherence. More details on Newmann et al.'s study and their empirical evidence from Chicago elementary schools will be presented in later sections. Similar to Newmann et al., Drake and Burns (2004) stated that "a coherent curriculum means that for teachers and students, the learning goals, activities, and assessments align with each other" (p. 19).

The Importance of Coherent Curriculum

Why do we need coherent curriculum? Why does the issue concern us? Researchers have commented on the incoherence of curriculum and its negative effects and on the positive effects associated with coherent curriculum.

Incoherent Curriculum

In 1980, Neil Postman emphasized the need for a coherent curriculum. Postman initially criticized the media's negative impacts on student learning and, particularly its fragmented, disconnected character—"nothing on television, for instance, has anything to do with anything else on television. There's no theme, coherence, or order to what is presented" (p. 302). He concluded that the media stressed instancy, discontinuity, immediate gratification, and emotion rather than constancy, coherence, deferred gratification, and analytical response. Postman suggested the schooling of our youth at all levels must avoid these biases. He cautioned that if the schools cannot assume this duty, no other organizations can, and suggested that "perhaps the most important contribution we can make to the education of our youth is to provide them with a sense of coherence in their studies" (p. 302). However, Postman observed that, in actuality, "at present, the typical high school or college curriculum reflects the fragmentation one finds in television's weekly schedule. Each subject, like each program, has nothing to do with any other" (p. 302).

The school curriculum lacks clarity and coherence is so serious a problem that "ambiguity tolerance" becomes a desirable trait for most educators (Steller, 1995). The American Association for the Advancement of Science (AAAS) (2001b) noted the repeated calls for broad changes in the curriculum during the 20th century reflected four persistent criticisms of the traditional curriculum, and two of them concerned curricular coherence: the first refers to both the lack of horizontal and vertical coherence by pointing out the fact that, "The curriculum is a mishmash of topics that lacks coherence across subject-matter domains and grade levels. It is some of this and some of that, with each piece being justified on its own without reference to a conceptual whole" (p. 3); while the second directs to the two consequences of curriculum change—shallowness and incoherence, because by adding too much new topics to the curriculum, the curriculum has become "grossly overstuffed with topics" (p. 4).

Based on their analysis of mathematics and science standards and textbooks, Schmidt, Houang, and Cougan (2002) characterized the U.S. curriculum as "highly repetitive, unfocused, unchallenging, and incoherent," especially in middle schools. This incoherent curriculum leads to teachers being required to teach content without depth. Although there are standards and enacted curricula, Schmidt et al. worried that they are "mile wide and an inch deep" (p. 3). Schmoker (2011b) also argued that a "reasonably coherent curriculum (what we teach)" is one of the three essentials for schools to improve student learning (the other two are "sound lessons" and "far more purposeful reading and writing in everyday discipline," see p. 2). However, they also suggested these three essential elements, as numerous studies demonstrate, are only rarely implemented.

Other researchers examined coherence with a broad perspective. For instance, Newmann, Smith, Allensworth, and Bryk (2001b) reviewed previous literature and discussion of coherence, and noted that "the idea of coherence often surfaces when educational researchers confront practices, programs, or policies found to be poorly conceived and coordinated or at odds with other practices, programs, and policies." (p. 298) This reminds us that the incoherence issue might exist beyond the traditional notion of curriculum.

The Negative Effect of Incoherent Curriculum

The question is what kind of impact an incoherent curriculum would produce upon student achievement. Over the years, researchers have provided empirical evidence regarding the impact of an incoherent curriculum on learning. For instance, Newmann, Smith, Allensworth, and Bryk (2001a) found "that unrelated, episodic programs undermine schools' capacity to boost student achievement," a conclusion that has been reported by quite a few other studies of school reform (e.g., Allington & Johnston, 1989; Ball & Cohen, 1996; Cohen, 1995; Hill & Celio, 1998; Newmann & Wehlage, 1995; O'Day, Goertz, & Floden, 1995; Smylie et al., 1998). Schmidt et al. (2002) analyzed the data from the Third International Math and Science Study (TIMSS) and found that American students and teachers are "greatly disadvantaged" by an incoherent math curriculum (and the texts, materials, and training that match it), while high-performing countries teach a very coherent math curriculum to their students. Based on Munson's (2011) analysis of nine countries that consistently outrank the U.S. on the Program for International Student Assessment (PISA) exam, Schmoker (2011a) concluded that a "coherent, liberal arts curriculum is the common denominator in the success of the highest-achieving countries" (p. 70).

The Positive Effect of Coherent Curriculum

Researchers in the previous section expressed concern about an incoherent curriculum and its negative impact on achievement. Researchers cited in this section, however, stress the positive outcomes derived from a coherent curriculum. Drake and Burns (2004) identified curricular coherence as a key factor for student success and as a critical factor in external evaluation. They understood curricular coherence in terms of curriculum alignment: "a coherent curriculum means that for teachers and students, the learning goals, activities, and assessments align with each other" (p. 19). Referring to Gordon's (2002) report of Chicago school reform, Drake and

Burns believed this alignment could better prepare students for both standardized tests and performance demonstrations. Silverman and Ennis (1996) also agreed that curricular coherence is essential to an effective and worthwhile curriculum. More similar evidences on the positive impact of coherent curriculum will be introduced in the "Best Practice" section.

Coherent Curriculum in Other Education Systems

The concept of coherent curriculum has gained worldwide attention. For instance, on the question "What can learners expect?," Education Scotland (2012)—the Scottish government agency responsible for supporting quality and improvement in learning and teaching from early years to adult and community education programs—argued that learners are entitled to, among other benefits, a coherent curriculum from 3 years of age to 18. Education Scotland emphasized that all children and young people are entitled to a coherent curriculum in which they can experience a smooth and well-paced progression through the experiences and outcomes, particularly across transitions (e.g., from pre-school to primary or from secondary school to college).

Other countries, such as China, have developed a coherent curriculum by (1) stipulating content standards for each subject at each grade, (2) developing designated sets of textbooks consistent with the standards, (3) compiling reference books for teachers on how to use the textbooks and providing pedagogical guidance, (4) implementing a test system to ensure that the contents are taught, and (5) producing a set of teaching practices that facilitate sharing among teachers (Shen, Poppink, Cui, & Fan, 2007; Shen, Zhen, & Poppink, 2007). Usiskin and Willmore (2008) compared the U.S. and Chinese mathematics textbooks and found that the U.S. textbooks have a complex design and broad range of topics, while the Chinese textbooks have a concise presentation and coherent organization.

Research Base

Current Status of the Literature on Coherent Curriculum

As discussed at the very beginning of this chapter, there are two major elements in the literature: (1) the notion of horizontal and vertical articulation within the curriculum and (2) the alignment among standards, curriculum, instruction, learning experience, assessment, etc. in a horizontally and vertically articulated curriculum.

These two concepts utilize a two-step process which principals could employ to promote, establish, and maintain coherent curricula: the first step is to work with the central office personnel and others to establish the horizontal and vertical articulation in curriculum, and the second is to go beyond the traditional notion of curriculum to align curriculum with instruction and assessment.

The Impact on Student Achievement: Whether and How?

Will coherent curriculum make a difference in student achievement? If so, what is the mechanism for making the difference? Researchers have tried to answer these questions from different viewpoints. Beane (1995) believed that a coherent curriculum opens possibilities for the integration of educational experiences. Beane argued that when curriculum is coherent, "young people are more likely to integrate educational experiences into their schemes of meaning, which in turn broadens and deepens their understanding of themselves and the world" (p. 4). In that sense, Beane concluded that a coherent curriculum could offer "unforgettable" experiences to students. Similarly, Pate, Homestead, and McGinnis (1997) contended that a coherent curriculum "encompasses meeting the needs of students and teachers, connecting the content, encouraging student voice, and relating schooling to real life, thereby ensuring that student learning is relevant and personally meaningful" (p. xiii).

Other researchers have claimed or explored either direct or indirect effects of a coherent curriculum on achievement. For instance, the Consortium on Chicago School Research conducted a number of studies to explore why some Chicago schools are improving while others are not (see Newmann, Smith, Allensworth, & Bryk, 2001a; 2001b). Their research revealed six features of improving schools and the first one is "improving schools have a coherent instructional program" (Gordon, 2002, p. 5). They found a strong positive relationship between instructional program coherence and student achievement. The specific research is available in Newmann, Smith, Allensworth, and Bryk (2001a; 2001b). As described by Gordon, Newmann et al. found schools that had no classrooms or only selected classrooms working on a coherent curriculum did not improve test scores. However, those schools that had a coherent schoolwide curriculum showed a 12% increase on the Iowa Test of Basic Skills (ITBS) test.

Another group of researchers also explored how curriculum coherence impacts student achievement. Based on the theory and research in the fields of learning, motivation, organizational productivity, and school effectiveness, Newmann et al. (2001a; 2001b) found that instructional program coherence could advance student achievement in two ways: it may lead to increased student engagement and learning, and it may help increase teachers' effectiveness (see 20001a, pp. 15–17; 2001b, pp. 300–301). Schmidt, Houang, & Cougan (2002) believed a coherent curriculum benefited students' achievement in three ways: it has a direct and positive influence on overall student achievement; it reduces students' differentiated achievement that derived from incoherent standards and curricula; finally, it weakens the link between student socioeconomic status and achievement.

Youngs, Holdgreve-Resendez, & Qian (2011) conducted interview research in seven elementary schools in two Michigan districts to investigate how instructional program coherence affects novice teachers' induction experiences. Participants who worked in schools with higher instructional program coherence had a higher quality of induction experiences.

Facilitations and Barriers in Developing and Maintaining Coherent Curriculum

Facilitators

What facilitators help schools achieve curricular coherence? Newmann et al. (2001b) identified the principal's instructional leadership, a clearly articulated instructional program framework, and organized resources as the most essential factors.

Newmann et al. (2001b) found that in schools with stronger instructional program coherence the principal advanced coherence by adopting or developing a school wide instructional program framework using either democratic or autocratic leadership. However, in those schools with less instructional program coherence, principals either failed to organize their instructional programs frameworks or provided "diffuse and uncoordinated instructional leadership or a clear lack of leadership" (p. 310). As a result, Newmann et al. concluded that "strong school-level leadership is central to the development of stronger instructional program coherence." Newmann et al. have used several schools as examples to illustrate their findings. Material from these examples is quoted in the "best practices" section of this chapter.

An external partner is another facilitating factor for curricular coherence (Newmann et al., 2001b). According to Newmann et al., during the grant period of the Chicago Annenberg Challenge, an external partner was appointed for each participating elementary school. The field study showed that an external partner can significantly advance a school's instructional program coherence. But Newmann and Sconzert (2000) also noticed that in some schools with low coherence, teachers were not aware that their school even had an external partner, and although some schools had multiple partners, they never really coordinated any activities (see Newmann & Sconzert, 2000). Just having partners is not a sufficient condition; school leaders must consider how to collaborate with their partners.

Newmann et al. (2001b) found that a school with coherent curriculum does not have to be small, possess more fiscal resources, or have a higher teacher–student ratio. Rather, these schools better utilize strategies to organize their available but limited resources and staff energy. Newmann et al. identified three such primary strategies.

The first strategy is significant investment in the instructional program. Newmann et al. noticed that schools with higher coherence invest substantially in school-wide instructional programs with corresponding staff training and fund well-trained coordinators who assist staff to implement their programs.

The second strategy is staff collaboration within instructional framework. Newmann et al. pointed out that higher coherence requires "extensive, continuing communication among teachers, mutual assistance, and working together to improve instruction according to the framework" (p. 312). They also noted that in more coherent schools, principals used several approaches to promote staff collaboration—common lesson-planning time (at grade levels and across grades), smaller clusters of teachers, and representative groups for school governance issues. The importance of staff collaboration is also articulated by Youngs, Holdgreve-Resendez, and Qian (2011).

The last strategy is coordination of community resources. Newmann et al. found that most principals work to coordinate community resources such as parental involvement, business partnerships, environmental projects, and museum and arts outings. However, the programs' impact on school instructional coherence is inconclusive. Schools with a more coherent curriculum are able to better coordinate community resources.

Barriers

Researchers identified barriers that discourage curricular coherence. The primary factors are (1) teachers' own experience and teacher education (Beane, 1995), (2) deep system and political difficulties (Schmidt, Wang, & McKnight, 2005), and (3) teachers' mental model that separates curriculum and instruction (Shen & Ma, 2006). Beane has already asked us, "Is it possible that we ourselves are unclear or do not know . . . what it is that the curriculum is all about? Can it be that the jigsaw puzzle metaphor describes not only the experience of young people in our schools, but also our own confusion about the curriculum?" (p. 1). This question implies it is possible that teachers, including curriculum writers, have an incomplete, fragmented experience. This is not only an issue for educators at schools but also for teacher education (Roth, 1999).

Schmidt and his colleagues (2005) identified two difficulties in pursuing a nationwide coherent curriculum—definition of what constitutes an "educational system" and identification of the institutional center that is to set curricular policies. Schmidt et al. (2005) concluded that the pursuit of curriculum coherence is much more difficult in the U.S. than in other countries, because the "U.S. has a long tradition of shared responsibility in curriculum decision-making as well as a complex decentralized arrangement for schooling and curriculum development" (p. 526).

The final barrier to coherent curriculum is that teachers hold "curriculum" and "instruction" to be two separate concepts. It is, therefore, very difficult to develop a coherent instructional program as advocated by Newmann et al. (2001a; 2001b). Shen and Ma (2006) conducted a study on the impact of systemic change on teaching practice using a large national data set. They reported that teachers' curricular practices are standardized to a certain extent under systemic change although their instructional practices remain varied and that "curriculum" and "instruction" are two separate concepts in teachers' mental models.

Best Practices

We have selected two cases to help principals and school improvement teams better understand why and how coherent curriculum works: the first example is a high school; the second concerns a school system reform effort.

Adlai E. Stevenson High School and Coherent Curriculum

According to Schmoker (2011b), Adlai Stevenson High School in Lincolnshire, Illinois, is one of the most successful and celebrated high schools in the United States and is the only high school in the state to receive four Blue Ribbon Awards for Excellence in Education from the U.S. Department of Education. *Newsweek* and *U.S. News and World Report* have ranked Stevenson among the top 100 high schools in America, with *Newsweek* selecting the school for the fourth time in 2005 (Kanold, 2005). For two decades, Stevenson has used the concept of a Common Coherent Curriculum to successfully educate its students. As a result, students at Stevenson made "immense, uninterrupted gains on every assessment administrated—standardized tests, end-of-course and end-of-quarter assessments, and AP exams" (Schmoker, 2011b, p. 65). For instance, the school increased its AP success rate by 800% (Schmoker, 2011b). Timothy Kanold is a former principal of Adlai E. Stevenson, where he served as Director of Mathematics and Science for over 20 years. Timothy Kanold talked about the elements of effective teaching at Stevenson: "Before we pursue new methods or programs or initiatives that consume huge amounts of precious time and money, we should focus on more deserving priorities: ensuring that a coherent curriculum is in place and being taught in schools where the essential elements of teaching are indeed routine components of every lesson" (Schmoker, 2011b, pp. 65–67).

Kanold (2005) also wrote a short article in which he shares the components, fundamental beliefs, and commitments that guide Stevenson and its curriculum. In order to provide readers with detailed information, the following is an excerpt from Kanold's article:

Common Coherent Curriculum

What does a common coherent curriculum look like?

In a school with a common coherent curriculum in all disciplines, the adults work collaboratively to ask several critical questions and continuously seek the answers.

Is the curriculum coherent?

A coherent curriculum effectively organizes and integrates important ideas so students can see how the ideas build on or connect with other ideas, enabling them to develop new understandings and skills. Without a clearly defined curriculum, teachers often duplicate their efforts and spend valuable class time on unnecessary review of the material students already know.

At Stevenson, there exists a teacher-developed, well-articulated curriculum that places an emphasis on important ideas and major themes over time. Is the curriculum focused on important content? School curricula must focus on content and instructional processes that are worth the time and attention of our students.

A focused, connected, coherent curriculum, in and of itself, is not the magic bullet or wonder drug that will remove the inequities that exist in schools. Although a focused, well-articulated, coherent curriculum is extremely important and should be required of all schools, it is not nearly enough.

The curriculum cannot flourish unless there exist individual opportunities to close the learning gap for each and every student. Without opportunities for teachers to work within a professional learning community or to collaborate on curriculum, instruction, and assessment issues, teachers new to a course will struggle.

> Without a school culture that seeks to place a premium on creating a learning culture for students and adults, the curriculum becomes lifeless and sterile. And without a community engaged in the support of a relevant and coherent curriculum, there exists little ownership in the school outside of its limited boundaries.
>
> To the public eye, the vision of a coherent curriculum is often invisible. Our focused effort, however, designed to avoid social injustices that might occur in student learning opportunities, has been a subtle but powerful part of our school culture visible to those within our community. It is what keeps us exemplary, yet unique.(Retrieved from http://www.beyond-the-book.com/leadership/leadership_082405.html, quoted with permission from Timothy Kanold)

Leadership and Instructional Program Coherence in Chicago Elementary Schools

In 1993, a group of Chicago school reform activists and education stakeholders worked together on a grant proposal, and in January 1995, the Annenberg Foundation awarded them a five-year grant of $49.2 million with an extra $100 million in private matching funds to establish the Chicago Annenberg Challenge.

The mission of this Challenge, according to Newmann et al. (2001a), was "to improve student learning by supporting intensive efforts to reconnect schools to their communities, restructure education, and improve classroom teaching" (p. 5). They decided to fund networks of schools and external partners that "seek to develop successful, community-based schools that address three critical education issues through whole-school change: school and teacher isolation, school size and personalism, and time for learning and improvement" (p. 5). As a result, during the grant period, more than half of Chicago's public elementary schools participated in this reform, and a variety of intervention programs were initiated with many external organizations involved. Consequently, researchers want to investigate "the extent to which schools channeled their efforts into coherent instructional programs and whether that, in tum, resulted in improved student achievement" (Newmann et al., 2001b, p. 302). Newmann et al. conducted an empirical research study and found that schools with higher instructional program coherence had better student performance in both reading and math performance (see Figure 6.1).

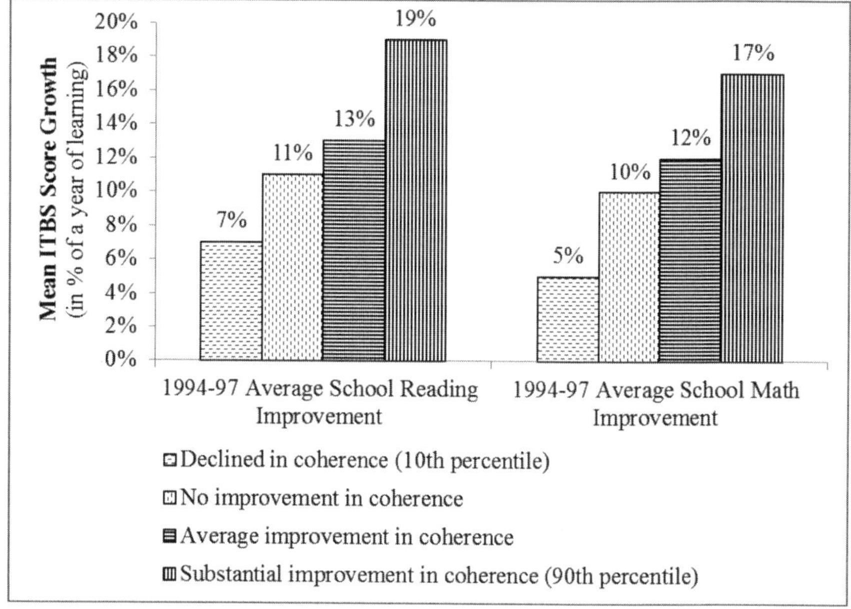

Figure 6.1 Coherence and Student Performance

*Source note: From "Instructional program coherence: What it is and why it should guide school improvement policy," by Newmann et al., 2001, *Educational Evaluation and Policy Analysis, 23*(4), p. 307. Copyright 2012 by Sage Publications. Reprinted with permission.

On the question of how schools achieved stronger instructional program coherence, Newmann et al. identified three key factors: sound school leadership, a clearly articulated instructional program framework, and organized school resources. To inspire other principals and school reformers, Newmann et al. (2001b) discussed in detail how leadership could foster a coherent instructional program in their schools:

School Leadership for an Instructional Framework

> Stronger instructional program coherence has been rooted in a principal's decision to adopt or develop a school wide instructional program framework and to make it a priority. We observed both democratic and autocratic approaches to leadership that advanced such frameworks. All of the principals of the high-scoring schools shared a conviction that a more common approach to instruction would assist student achievement. Noted one principal, "You will not have an effect if

> you are just working with five or six teachers; you have to have 20 teachers to make a difference."
>
> In two of the highest-scoring schools, Chelsea and Ackerman, principals led staff to collectively adapt and refine an instructional program framework. For four years Chelsea's principal worked with an external partner and with teacher leaders to implement a framework for literacy diagnosis, development, and assessment based on the Reading Recovery program. . . .
>
> Not every school developed instructional frameworks democratically. In Bishop, and to a lesser extent Hartford and Larkin, principals or administrative teams mandated that teachers use purchased frameworks; teacher responses were mixed. Nonetheless, those schools had highly to moderately coordinated instructional programs emphasizing shared instructional strategies and assessments, as well as sustained staff development aimed at consistent implementation of the frameworks. (pp. 306–310)

Summary

Several factors can advance curricular coherence: (1) principal leadership (to develop, adapt, or refine the common instructional framework; and to implement the common instructional framework);(2) teacher collaboration around the common instructional framework; (3) professional development for teachers around the common instructional framework; (4) external partnership; and (5) organization of exiting school resource (investing in instructional programs and staff training, fostering staff collaboration within instructional framework, and coordinating community resources to support the program). Also, we noted that the concept of coherent curriculum entails both the traditional notion of horizontal and vertical articulation within the curriculum and aligning curriculum with instruction, learning experience, assessment, etc. The mechanisms with which coherent curriculum could advance student achievement include increasing teacher's teaching effectiveness, enhancing student engagement, and improving new teachers' induction experience. The literature on how to develop curricular coherence and how the curricular coherence could impact student achievement have been summarized and visualized in Figure 6.2.

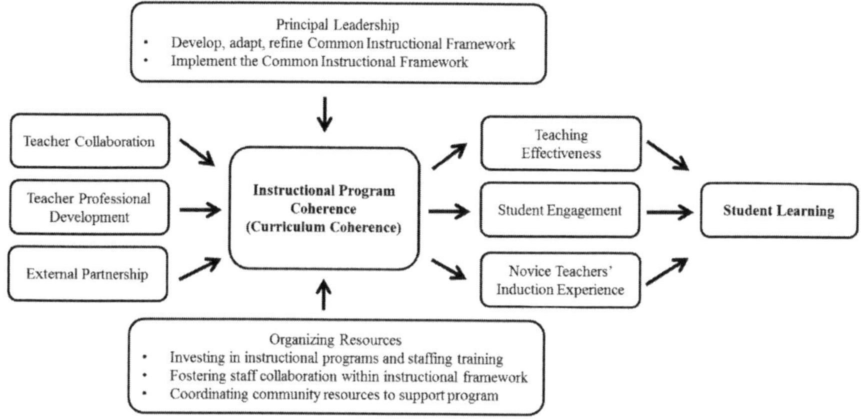

Figure 6.2 How Coherent Curriculum Advances Student Learning

Resources

A Curriculum Mapping Process for Coherent Curriculum

The Center for Collaborative Education (2001) compiled the *Guide to Curriculum Development*, in which five principles of curriculum development were introduced. The fifth principle was "A coherent curriculum should be developed across the entire school" (p. iii). In order to build curricular coherence, a Curriculum Mapping Process was developed in which four guiding questions were asked—"What do we want our students to know and be able to do?"; "What are we currently teaching?"; "Where are the redundancies and the gaps between what we should be teaching, and what we are teaching?"; and "What will we do about these redundancies and gaps?" (p. 12).

Project 2061: Its Research, Publications, and Evaluations on Curriculum Coherence

According to its online introduction (http://www.project2061.org/about), Project 2061 is a long-term initiative of the American Association for the Advancement of Science (AAAS) to help all Americans become literate in science, mathematics, and technology. One of the tasks that Project 2061 engages in is to develop tools for evaluating curricular coherence. The following are some key dimensions along which to evaluate curricular coherence: (1) alignment with a coherent set of ideas, (2) connections between the ideas of science and phenomena in the natural world, (3) connections to prerequisite and other related ideas, (4) connections to evidence supporting the idea, and (5) avoidance of nonessential information. Please see Roseman, Linn, and Koppal (2008, pp. 16–25) for more information. More details of its research reports and publications can be found on the website.

Annotated Bibliography of Suggested Readings

American Association for the Advancement of Science. (1989). *Science for all Americans.* New York: Oxford University Press. The book, the first publication of Project 2061, defines science literacy, presents a coherent story of the knowledge, skills, and habits of mind that constitute science literacy, and stipulates some principles for effective learning and teaching.

American Association for the Advancement of Science. (1993). *Benchmarks for science literacy.* New York: Oxford University Press. The book states what all students should know and be able to do in science, mathematics, and technology by the end of grades 2, 5, 8, and 12 and thus unpacks the coherent story presented in *Science for all Americans* into sequential grade-level steps that lead toward science literacy.

American Association for the Advancement of Science. (2001a). *Atlas of science literacy.* Washington, DC: American Association for the Advancement of Science. The two-volume collection of conceptual-strand maps helps educators distribute responsibilities for students' science learning across different grades and subjects, thus fostering K–12 curricular coherence.

American Association for the Advancement of Science. (2001b). *Designs for science literacy.* New York: Oxford University Press. The book and its companion CD-ROM *Designs on Disk*, deal with the critical issues involved in assembling quality instructional materials into a coherent K–12 curriculum.

Beane, J. A. (1995). *Toward a coherent curriculum: 1995 yearbook of the Association for Supervision and Curriculum Development.* Alexandria, VA: The Association. The book addresses issues relevant to the development of a coherent curriculum, which include introduction of a coherent curriculum and the search for coherence across and beyond the subject areas.

Kali, Y., Linn, M. C., & Roseman, J. E. (2008). *Designing coherent science education: Implications for curriculum, instruction, and policy.* New York: Teachers College Press. The book focuses attention on the interrelated nature of science knowledge and on strategies for supporting learners as they develop their science literacy.

Newmann, F., Smith, B., Allensworth, E., & Bryk, A. S. (2001b). Instructional program coherence: What it is and why it should guide school improvement policy. *Educational Evaluation and Policy Analysis, 23*(4), 297–321. The article presents the concept of instructional program coherence and explains why school improvement frameworks that incorporate instructional program coherence are more likely to enhance student achievement than multiple, unrelated initiatives.

References

Allington, R. L., & Johnston, P. (1989). Coordination, collaboration, and consistency: The redesign of compensatory and special education interventions. In R. E. Slavin, N. L. Karweit, & N. A. Madden (Eds.), *Effective programs for students at risk* (pp. 320–354). Needham Heights, MA: Allyn and Bacon.

American Association for the Advancement of Science. (1989). *Science for all Americans.* New York: Oxford University Press.

American Association for the Advancement of Science. (1993). *Benchmarks for science literacy.* New York: Oxford University Press.

American Association for the Advancement of Science. (2001a). *Atlas of science literacy.* Washington, DC: American Association for the Advancement of Science.

American Association for the Advancement of Science. (2001b). *Designs for science literacy.* New York: Oxford University Press.

Ball, D., & Cohen, D. (1996). Reform by the book: What is: Or might be: The role of curriculum materials in teacher learning and instructional reform? *Educational Researcher, 25*(9), 6–8, 14.

Beane, J. A. (1995). *Toward a coherent curriculum: 1995 yearbook of the Association for Supervision and Curriculum Development.* Alexandria, VA: Association for Supervision and Curriculum Development.

Center for Collaborative Education. (2001). *Guide to curriculum development.* Boston, MA: Center for Collaborative Education. Retrieved October 15, 2012 from http://www.turningpts.org/pdf/Curriculum.pdf

Cohen, David K. (1995). What is the system in systemic reform? *Educational Researcher, 24*(9), 11–17, 31.

Drake, S. M., & Burns, R. C. (2004). *Meeting standards through integrated curriculum.* Alexandria, VA: Association for Supervision and Curriculum Development.

Education Scotland. (2012). *A coherent curriculum.* Retrieved October 15, 2012 from http://www.educationscotland.gov.uk/thecurriculum/whatcanlearnersexpect/coherentcurriculum.asp

Gordon, D. T. (2002). Moving instruction to center stage. *Harvard Education Letter, 18*(5), 5–7.

Hill, P. T., & Celio, M. B. (1998). *Fixing urban schools.* Washington, DC: Brookings Institution Press.

Johnson, R. K. (1989). *The second language curriculum.* Cambridge, England: Cambridge University Press.

Kanold, T. D. (2005). *A common coherent curriculum.* Retrieved October 15, 2012 from http://www.beyond-the-book.com/leadership/leadership_082405.html

Munson, L. (2011). What students really need to learn. *Educational Leadership, 68*(6), 10–14.

Newmann, F., Smith, B., Allensworth, E., & Bryk, A. (2001a). *School instructional program coherence: Benefits and challenges.* Chicago, IL: Consortium on Chicago School Research. Retrieved October 15, 2012 from http://ccsr.uchicago.edu/sites/default/files/publications/p0d02.pdf

Newmann, F., Smith, B., Allensworth, E., & Bryk, A. S. (2001b). Instructional program coherence: What it is and why it should guide school improvement policy. *Educational Evaluation and Policy Analysis, 23*(4), 297–321.

Newmann, F. M., & Sconzert, K. (2000). *School improvement with external partners.* Chicago, IL: Consortium on Chicago School Research.

Newmann, F. M., & Wehlage, G. G. (1995). *Successful school restructuring: A report to the public and educators by the Center on Organization and Restructuring of Schools.* Madison, WI: Wisconsin Center for Education Research.

O'Day, J. A., Goertz, M. E., & Floden, R. E. (1995). *Building capacity for education reform* (CPRE Policy Briefs: Reporting on Issues and Research in Education Policy, RB-18). New Brunswick, NJ: Consortium for Policy Research in Education.

Pate, P. E., Homestead, E. R., & McGinnis, K. L. (1997). *Making integrated curriculum work: Teachers, students, and the quest for coherent curriculum.* New York: Teachers College Press.

Postman, N. (1980). The ascent of humanity: A coherent curriculum. *Educational Leadership, 37*(4), 300–303.

Roseman, J. E., Linn, M. C., & Koppal, M. (2008). Characterizing curriculum coherence. In Y. Kali, M. C. Linn, & J. E. Roseman (Eds.), *Designing coherent science education* (pp. 13–38). New York: Teachers College Press.

Roth, R. A. (1999). *The role of the university in the preparation of teachers.* London: Falmer.

Schmidt, W. H., Houang, R., & Cougan, L. (2002). A coherent curriculum: The case of mathematics. *American Educator, 26*(2), 10–26, 47–48.

Schmidt, W. H., Wang, H. C., & McKnight, C. C. (2005). Curriculum coherence: An examination of U.S. mathematics and science content standards from an international perspective. *Journal of Curriculum Studies, 37*(5), 525–559.

Schmoker, M. J. (2011a). Curriculum now. *Phi Delta Kappan, 93*(3), 70–71.

Schmoker, M. J. (2011b). *Focus: Elevating the essentials to radically improve student learning.* Alexandria, VA: ASCD.

Shen, J., & Ma, X. (2006). Does systemic change work? Curricular and instructional practice in the context of systemic change. *Leadership and Policy in Schools, 5*(3), 231–256.

Shen, J., Poppink, S., Cui, Y., & Fan, G. (2007). Lesson planning: A practice of professional responsibility and development. *Educational Horizons, 85*(4), 248–258.

Shen, J., Zhen, J., & Poppink, S. (2007). Open lessons: A practice to develop a learning community for teachers. *Educational Horizons, 85*(3), 181–191.

Shwartz, Y., Weizman, A., Fortus, D., & Krajcik, J. (2008). The IQWST experience: Using coherence as a design principle for a middle school science curriculum. *The Elementary School Journal, 109*(2), 199–219.

Silverman, S. J., & Ennis, C. D. (1996). *Student learning in physical education: Applying research to enhance instruction.* Champaign, IL: Human Kinetics.

Smith, M. S., & O'Day, J. (1991). Systemic school reform. In S. H. Fuhrman & B. Malen (Eds.), *The politics of curriculum and testing: The 1990 Yearbook of the Politics of Education Association* (pp. 233–267). London: Falmer.

Smylie, M. A., Bilcer, D. K., Kochanek, J., Sconzert, K., Shipps, D., & Swyers, H. (1998). *Getting started: A first look at Chicago Annenberg schools and networks.* Chicago: Consortium on Chicago School Research.

Steller, A. W. (1995). Foreword. In Beane, J. A. (Ed.), *Toward a coherent curriculum: 1995 yearbook of the Association for Supervision and Curriculum Development.* Alexandria, VA: The Association.

Usiskin, Z., & Willmore, E. (2008). *Mathematics curriculum in Pacific Rim countries—China, Japan, Korea, and Singapore: Proceedings of a conference.* Charlotte, NC: Information Age.

Youngs, P., Holdgreve-Resendez, R., & Qian, H. (2011). The role of instructional program coherence in beginning elementary teachers' induction experiences. *The Elementary School Journal, 111*(3), 455–476.

7

Real-Time and Embedded Instructional Assessment

DENNIS C. McCRUMB AND ROBERT J. LENEWAY

Introduction

When considering the topic of instructional assessment of student performance, most people immediately think of tests—unit or chapter tests or final exams. Too often student assessments are considered a final analysis of student learning, ultimately leading to a grade (Kimball & Cone, 2002). In fact, assessment is an enormous topic including everything from nationally normed standardized tests, statewide accountability tests, district benchmark tests, and daily classroom tests (Garrison & Ehringhaus, 2011).

Traditionally, standardized, norm-referenced achievement tests have provided school districts with data which indicated the overall success of their educational programs. More recently, school reform efforts have driven schools to administer standard-based benchmarked assessments throughout the year to determine whether students are meeting the state or district benchmarks (Stecker, Lembke, & Foegen, 2008).

These traditional types of tests do little to provide information on how students are actually progressing toward curriculum goals. Rather, these graded tests put pressure on students to do well so they can earn a specific score. It was believed that this pressure motivated students to get good grades and thus increased learning (Stiggins, 2005), but this conjecture assumes all students are motivated by pressure to excel academically. As students progress through school they either understand curricular concepts and are successful, or they do not grasp them and fall further and further behind each year (Stiggins, 2005). Because of this, struggling students view themselves as failures and feel a sense of hopelessness. Some teachers insist that they taught the material, but the student just did not learn. These teachers take little responsibility for student learning. Stiggins (2005) asserts the following: "Assessment and grading procedures designed to permit only a few students to succeed must now be revised to permit the possibility that all students could succeed at some appropriate level" (p. 326).

Before discussing the various types of assessments, the purpose of assessing instruction should be reviewed. Kellough and Kellough (1998, pp. 418–419) characterize seven purposes of instructional assessment:

- To assist student learning
- To identify students' strengths and weaknesses
- To assess the effectiveness of a particular instructional strategy
- To assess and improve the effectiveness of curriculum programs
- To assess and improve teaching effectiveness
- To provide data that assist in decision making
- To communicate with and involve parents

Kellough and Kellough (1998) go on to state that students must have answers to the following basic questions:

- Where am I going?
- Where am I now?
- How do I get where I am going?
- How will I know when I get there?
- Am I on the right track for getting there?

These same questions are the basis for professional learning communities.

Ubben, Hughes, and Norris (2011, p. 134) assert "Learning environments should be assessment centered. Assessments are to be formative to provide teachers with timely information from which they can modify instructional planning to better accomplish learning objectives. The assessment must be to measure if the students are learning for understanding. Testing should be frequent (daily or weekly). The purpose of the tests should be to give feedback to both students and teachers."

The American Association for Higher Education (AAHE) has established nine principles for implementing instructional assessments (Pausch & Popp, 1997). They are:

- The assessment of student learning begins with educational values.
- Assessment is most effective when it reflects an understanding of learning as multidimensional, integrated, and revealed in performance over time.
- Assessment works best when the programs it seeks to improve have clear, explicitly stated purposes.
- Assessment requires attention to outcomes but also and equally to the experiences that lead to those outcomes.
- Assessment works best when it is ongoing, not episodic.
- Assessment fosters wider improvement when representatives from across the educational community are involved.
- Assessment makes a difference when it begins with issues of use and illuminates questions that people really care about.
- Assessment is most likely to lead to improvement when it is part of a larger set of conditions that promote change.
- Through assessment educators meet responsibilities to students.

Marzano (2010) defines three types of classroom assessment as obtrusive, unobtrusive, and student generated. During obtrusive assessments little learning takes place. The most common example would be paper and pencil tests. Unobtrusive assessments do not interrupt the flow of instruction, and often students do not even know they are being assessed. Most unobtrusive assessments occur through teacher observation of student performance on instructional tasks. Student-generated assessments are just that—students suggest ways that they can demonstrate their mastery of course content.

Many types of instructional assessments exist, including performance, project, portfolio, observation as well as formative and summative assessments. The assessments can also be norm referenced or criterion referenced. Norm referenced refers to assessments that compare a student to other students. Criterion-referenced tests compare student work to a set of objectives, standards, or outcomes. In the review of real-time, embedded instructional assessments, the emphasis and focus will primarily revolve around formative assessments in comparison to summative assessments.

Literature Base

Comparing Formative vs. Summative Assessments

Summative assessments generally are used to assess what students know or do not know at any particular time (Garrison & Ehringhaus, 2011). Chappuis and Chappuis (2007) offer the following definition. "In general, its results are used to make some sort of judgment, such as to determine what grade a student will receive on a classroom assignment, measure program effectiveness, or determine whether a school has made adequate yearly progress. Summative assessment, sometimes referred to as assessment of learning, typically documents how much learning has occurred at a point in time; its purpose is to measure the level of student, school, or program success" (p. 14). Examples of summative assessments include state assessments, district benchmark or interim assessments, unit or chapter tests, and scores that are used for accountability of schools (AYP) and students (Garrison & Ehringhaus, 2011).

A definition offered by Popham (2008) indicates formative assessment is a planned process in which assessment-elicited evidence of students' status is used by teachers to adjust their ongoing instructional procedures or by students to adjust their current learning tactics. Garrison and Ehringhaus (2011) view formative assessments as providing the information necessary to adjust teaching and learning while they are happening.

In essence, summative assessments judge student knowledge at the end of a learning cycle with a grade or rating, while formative assessments provide data during the learning cycle so adjustments can be made to enhance learning, and these assessments are not graded.

The Popularity of Formative Assessments

Formative assessments are becoming increasingly popular because educators are realizing that summative tests are not given often enough to affect the daily or even weekly curricular and instructional decisions. They do not provide evidence of each individual student's mastery of required standards or objectives (Stiggens, 2005). Research into one or more of the strategies, practices, and techniques included in the formative assessment process began in the early 1970s—making formative assessment the most researched assessment practice today. The recent interest in formative assessment received traction in the United States with the publication and subsequent sharing of the 1998 *Phi Delta Kappan* article "Inside the Black Box: Raising Standards through Classroom Assessment" by the United Kingdom's Dylan Wiliam and Paul Black. Some confusion exists among educators about the definition of formative assessment, since many test publishers use the term in association with their off-the-shelf products. This chapter views formative assessment as an instructionally embedded process, adhering to definitions developed by the Council of Chief State School Officers (Black & Wiliam, 1998).

Research has shown that formative assessments when implemented properly provide dramatic gains in learning. The work of Black and Wiliam (1998) found that the gains in learning by using formative assessments were amongst the largest ever reported for educational interventions. Formative assessment works. There is no particular formula to follow. According to Black and Wiliam (1988), all types of formative assessments trigger student learning.

It also appears to work very well for slow learners (Popham, 2008). Many studies have arrived at an important conclusion—that improved formative assessment helps low achievers more than other students and, therefore, reduces the range of achievement while raising achievement overall (Brookhart, 2008). A notable recent example is a study devoted entirely to low-achieving students and students with learning disabilities which shows that frequent assessment feedback helps both groups enhance their learning (Bakula, 2010). Using formative assessment gives students a second chance to learn material they did not master the first time around. It lets failure become a learning experience rather than something to fear.

Marzano (2010) explains the elements of formative assessment as defined by Popham (2008) as follows:

- It is a process, not any particular test.
- It is used not just by teachers, but by both teachers and students.
- Formative assessment takes place during instruction.
- It provides assessment-based feedback to teachers and students.

The function of this feedback is to help teachers and students make adjustments that will improve students' achievement of intended curricular aims.

Feedback as Part of Formative Assessment

Effective feedback is critical in the formative assessment process. Students need to know what skills and knowledge they are to gain, how close they arc to achieving those skills, and what they need to do next in order to be a successful learner. Brookhart (2008) states that formative feedback can provide cognitive interventions and motivate students to succeed at the same time. Once students understand what they are to learn and achieve the learning goals, most students then feel they have control over their learning and are motivated to gain further success. Marzano (2003) states that some students are driven to succeed while others will do anything they can to avoid failure, which means they may choose to not even try to learn.

Hattie and Timperley (2007) have created a model of feedback that incorporates four levels:

1. Feedback about the task—whether answers are right or wrong or directions to get more information.
2. Feedback about the processing of the task—strategies used or strategies that could be used.
3. Feedback about self-regulation—feedback about student self-evaluation or self-confidence.
4. Feedback about the student as a person.

Based on feedback research and theory, Marzano (2003) has drawn the following generalizations on the best ways to use feedback.

1. Feedback should be "corrective" in nature—provide students with an explanation of what they did right and wrong.
2. Feedback should be timely—immediately following an assessment.
3. Feedback should be specific to a criterion—it should reference a specific level or skill or knowledge.
4. Students can effectively provide some of their own feedback—by keeping track of their performance as learning occurs.

As seen above Marzano (2003) has indicated that feedback must be based on criteria or goals. He has also synthesized three generalizations from the research on goal setting.

1. Instructional goals narrow what students focus on.
2. Instructional goals should not be too specific.
3. Students should be encouraged to personalize the teacher's goals.

Brookhart (2008) views goals in terms of "learning targets and criteria." She states that teachers must be sure to do the following with each assignment (p. 72).

- Require student work to demonstrate the content knowledge or skills specified in the learning target.
- Require students to demonstrate the cognitive process specified in the learning target.
- Provide students with complete and clear directions.
- Specify the criteria for good work (which will become the criteria for both feedback and final evaluation).

Feedback Strategies and Content

It is critical that teachers provide students with the proper feedback and in an appropriate manner. Brookhart (2008) summarized the research and makes recommendations for feedback strategies and content based on the research. The recommendations are delineated in Table 7.1 (2008, pp. 5–7):

Table 7.1. Feedback Recommendations

Strategies	Recommendations
Timing	• Provide immediate feedback for knowledge of facts • Delay feedback slightly for more comprehensive reviews of student thinking and processing • Never delay feedback beyond when it would make a difference to students • Provide feedback as often as is practical, for all major assignments
Amount	• Prioritize—pick the most important points • Choose points that relate to major learning goals • Consider the student's developmental level
Mode	• Select the best mode for the message. Would a comment in passing the student's desk suffice? Is a conference needed? • Interactive feedback is best • Give written feedback on written work • Use demonstration if how to do something is an issue
Audience	• Individual feedback makes the student feel the teacher values their learning • Group/class feedback works if most of the class missed the concept—re-teaching opportunity

Content	Recommendations
Focus	• When possible, describe both the work and the process • Comment on the student's self-regulation if the comment will foster self-efficacy • Avoid personal comments
Comparison	• Use criterion-referenced feedback for giving information about the work itself • Use norm-referenced for giving information about student processes or effort • Use self-referenced for unsuccessful learners who need to see the progress they are making, not how far they are from the goal
Function	• Describe • Don't judge
Valence	• Use positive comments that describe what was done well • Accompany negative descriptions of the work with positive suggestions for improvement
Clarity	• Use vocabulary and concepts the student will understand • Tailor the amount and content of feedback to the student's developmental level
Specificity	• Make the degree of specificity to the student and the task • Make feedback specific enough that they know what to do but not so specific that it is done for them • Identify errors or types of errors, but do not correct every one—leave some for the student to correct
Tone	• Choose words that communicate respect for the student and the work • Choose words that position the student as the agent • Choose words that cause students to think or wonder

*Source Note: From *How to Give Effective Feedback to Your Students* (pp. 5–7), Susan M. Brookhart. Alexandria, VA: ASCD. (c) 2008 by ASCD. Reprinted with permission. Learn more about ASCD at *www.ascd.org*

Feedback for Different Types of Learners

Successful Students. Students who are successful typically are interested in both school and learning and want to do well on assignments. They also greatly benefit from constructive feedback on their skills and knowledge. These students do self-assessments spontaneously whether or not the teacher provides opportunities for this activity (Brookhart, 2008).

Teachers may often neglect to provide feedback to these successful students in order to spend more time with slower learners. Successful students are going to learn even without teacher feedback. Brookhart (2008) warns teachers not to fall into this trap. Successful students will achieve even more with proper feedback. No student should be neglected by the teacher even though they are perceived as successful.

Struggling Students. Struggling students are those who have fallen behind in school or have not had positive learning experiences. "Struggling students will benefit from feedback that helps them connect the process they used with the results they obtained" (Brookhart, p. 99). These students struggle when they view the large gap in their knowledge based on criteria. Therefore, criterion-referenced feedback is not the best choice for these students.

Self-referenced is much more applicable—comparing their current work to previous work. It is important to make suggestions for improvement in small steps for struggling students. Break complex tasks into small manageable steps. Gradual and small improvements are better for the students than being overwhelmed and not improving at all (Brookhart, 2008).

Reluctant Students. According to Brookhart (2008), "Students who perceive themselves as failures are accustomed to viewing any kind of feedback as confirmation that they are stupid" (p. 106). All they hear is what they did wrong. The natural tendency for teachers is to do just that, tell the students what they did wrong. This method and message provide constant confirmation in their minds that they cannot learn and, in turn, makes them not willing to put forth any effort.

As with struggling students, reluctant students will also benefit from self-referenced assessments. Compare the work the student is currently doing to his or her previous work. Make suggestions in small increments. This may take more time, but when students see success and progress, they become more willing to put forth effort into the learning process.

Assessing Teacher Performance

A critical dimension of student learning and achievement is the quality of the classroom teacher. Many states including Illinois and Michigan have passed legislation requiring increased teacher accountability. In these instances, part of the teacher evaluation process includes a component of student achievement. Teachers are being held accountable for student success as part of their job performance assessment. Therefore, it is important to utilize a teacher evaluation process that aims for improving teacher performance. Both Danielson (1996) and Marshall (2009) state that teacher evaluations should be both summative and formative. These evaluations should be based on many classroom observations, mini-unannounced observations and face-to-face conversations with teachers. Formative feedback will allow teachers the opportunity to immediately alter their strategies for providing instruction.

The key component to quality teacher evaluation is the building principal. Some principals do not like to provide proper feedback or criticism because they do not want to hurt the teacher's feelings. Therefore, they give inflated scores to underperforming teachers. Marshall (2009) indicates that this does not help teachers improve. The kindest thing a principal can do for an underperforming teacher is give candid, evidence-based feedback, listen to the teacher's concerns, and provide robust follow-up support (Marshall 2009). Feeney (2007) states that the end goal of any evaluation should be increased student learning. Teacher evaluation should provide constructive feedback to support teachers' professional growth, and it should screen out unqualified teachers. Teacher evaluation should not be a once-or-twice-a-year event, but should be enhanced through providing feedback throughout the school year. Feeney goes on to state that evaluation feedback should contain the following elements:

- Feedback should be based on descriptive observable data.
- Feedback should provide characteristics of effective teaching.
- Feedback should promote reflective inquiry and self-directedness to foster improvements.

Many teacher evaluation programs have been developed to assist principals with the task of assessing teacher performance. Marshall (2009) has developed a teacher evaluation rubric organized around six domains covering all aspects of a teacher's job performance. They include:

A. Planning and preparation for learning
B. Classroom management
C. Delivery of instruction
D. Monitoring, assessment, and follow-up
E. Family and community outreach
F. Professional responsibilities

Each of these domains contains 10 subcategories against which the teacher is evaluated. The rubric uses a four-level rating scale with the following labels:

4. Expert
3. Proficient
2. Needs Improvement
1. Does Not Meet Standards

Charlotte Danielson (1996) created a very detailed teacher evaluation rubric by dividing the complex activity of teaching into 24 components clustered into four domains of teaching responsibility. The components of each domain contain smaller elements for evaluating teachers. Teachers are rated against each of the smaller elements as "unsatisfactory," "basic," "proficient" or "distinguished." The domains and components are listed below:

Domain 1: Preparation and Planning

- Demonstrating knowledge of content and pedagogy
- Demonstrating knowledge of students
- Selecting instructional goals
- Demonstrating knowledge of resources
- Designing coherent instruction
- Assessing student learning

Domain 2: The Classroom Environment

- Creating an environment of respect and rapport
- Establishing a culture of learning
- Managing classroom procedures
- Managing student behavior
- Organizing physical space

Domain 3: Instruction

- Communicating clearly and accurately
- Using questioning and discussion techniques
- Engaging students in learning
- Providing feedback to students
- Demonstrating flexibility and responsiveness

Domain 4: Professional Responsibilities

- Reflecting on teaching
- Maintaining accurate records
- Communicating with families
- Contributing to the school and district
- Growing and developing professionally
- Showing professionalism

Best Practice

Formative Evaluation and Motivation

Students must be positively motivated in order to be successful learners. Marzano (2003) has developed four action steps to enhance student motivation based on his meta-analysis of motivation research:

Action Step 1: Provide students with feedback on their knowledge gain.

Action Step 2: Provide students with tasks and activities that are inherently engaging.

Action Step 3: Provide opportunities for students to construct and work on long-term projects of their own design.

Action Step 4: Teach students about the dynamics of motivation and how those dynamics affect them.

Effective Planning

It is clear from the research that if teachers have effective planning skills, the probability of improved student achievement increases. Ubben, Hughes and Norris (2011) provides the following process for assuring teacher preparedness.

1. Identify instructional objectives.
2. Set an appropriate level of difficulty for mastery.
3. Plan out matching instructional methods, procedures, materials, and student activities.
4. Use good formative and summative evaluation techniques. (p. 135)

A Vignette of Best Practice[1]

Pat, an assistant superintendent for curriculum and instruction, had a legitimate concern with student achievement in the district's elementary schools in a medium-sized urban center with a very diverse population. Literally, on one side of the railroad tracks the residents were very poor and mostly minorities. On the other side of the tracks lived the more economically advantaged. The schools in these areas reflected the population in general, and test scores in the elementary schools in the poor part of town were far below those in the wealthier section.

Learning communities were implemented and professional development opportunities were provided for teachers, but scores in the poor-area schools remained below the wealthier schools. As Pat was reviewing the individual classroom scores for the past two years, she discovered some startling results. One classroom teacher in a poor-area elementary school was seeing dramatic increases in student achievement. These students were beginning to surpass the students from the wealthier part of town. Even more interesting was the fact that this particular teacher was only in her third year. Pat went to this teacher to find out what she was doing which led to large increases in student achievement. She discovered that the teacher utilized the following eight-step approach to her instructional methodology.

1. Pre-test and review data
2. Create time lines for instruction
3. Utilize direct instructional techniques
4. Regular assessment—1 to 3 weeks
5. Re-teach when appropriate
6. Enrichment for those not needing re-teaching
7. Maintenance of concepts learned
8. Constant monitoring of student achievement

Pat provided training on this procedure for the remainder of the teachers in that building resulting in increased student achievement and test scores. This elementary school using this instructional process became the highest-achieving school in the district.

Embedded Assessment Tools

Many new programs and tools are or have recently become available to assist the teacher. Marzano (2003) says that the key issue about using technology in the classroom is that the users must be familiar enough with the technology that they are able to make proper assessments when utilizing such tools. Miranda (2007) also points to district and school level factors such as funding, leadership, vision, and technology planning on the degree of use of instructional technologies. Other research (Anderson & Dexter, 2005; Dawson & Rakes, 2003; Russell et al., 2003) claims that principal leadership, availability of professional development for principals, especially when it is focused on technology integration and perceived pressure to use technology to be among "the most important contributors to teacher and student's use of technology" (Miranda & Russell, 2011, p. 312). The following are a few examples of several of the more promising emerging embedded assessment tools.

White Boards. According to Wikipedia, "an interactive whiteboard (IWB) is a large interactive display that connects to a computer and projector. A projector projects the computer's desk top onto the board's surface where users control the computer using a pen, finger, stylus, or other device." See http://tinyurl.com/9kvlcrt.

Marzano (2003) reports that the interactive white board seems to be excellent for providing feedback when conducting an embedded assessment as it helps the students observe themselves as well as their peers. His research has shown that there has been "sustainable improvement in student achievement" using this type of technology. Feedback that is corrective, direct, and specific is the most helpful. According to Marzano, learning from peers is one of the most effective methods of providing information even when doing an assessment because the peer-to-peer interaction can be less intimidating.

Quizlet. One popular free embedded assessment internet tool is Quizlet, which makes or finds online flashcards made by others. Quizlet lets students familiarize themselves with the material while keeping track of their scores and retesting any incorrect answers. For the teacher, it can generate customizable tests with short-answer, matching, multiple choice, and true/false options. It can be shared with friends, includes a game mode, and is available on mobile phone and other portable devices.

Infographics. Our students, among the youngest members of this "graphics" or, more accurately, "multimedia" world, are surrounded by images—on buildings, billboards, in magazines, on TV, in films, and in computer games—which they also often passively absorb. The messages and values conveyed by these images define norms and ideals of dress, behavior, and beliefs including future career choices. In comparison with their earlier counterparts, contemporary American students are probably far more comfortable with, place greater value on, and derive much of their knowledge from images—as opposed to text. Little wonder that so many of our students are visual learners.

Teaching these days involves competing with marvelous electronic gadgets—from the enhanced televisions and smart phones to the Xbox 360—as well as with all the time students spend watching and using them. Student experience seems to have become so much more visual in nature that educators can't compete using the same tools we used when we were our students' age. Given the amount of information students now get visually, the ability to communicate and understand through visual means—visual literacy—is becoming increasingly important.

According to Schrock (2011), "Infographics are traditionally viewed as visual elements such as signs, charts, maps, or diagrams that aid comprehension of a given text-based content." The charts and graphs seen on the front page of U.S. newspapers are examples of synthesizing large amounts of statistics data into easy to understand visual images. This process can provide an engaging and effective means to quickly assess student critical thinking and understanding of discovered data and the salient issue(s) supported by that data, much more than is possible in any multi-response test or essay.

Often more powerful than words or imagery alone, infographics utilize visual elements of design and words to convey a message in such a way that context, meaning, and understanding are transcended to the observer in a manner not previously experienced. However, since the days fire first evolved we've been using infographics, as visual shorthand to convey information to the viewer or readers that might take paragraphs or pages to explain in words. It is not easy to represent the whole story in one single page or paragraph with a visual image but it is far more effective than reading an entire book (Schrock, 2011).

ASSISTment. A free web-based platform that allows teachers to write individual ASSISTments (composed of questions and associated hints, solutions, web-based videos, etc.) is another example of an internet-supplied assessment tool. The word "ASSISTment" blends tutoring "assistance" with "assessment" reporting to teachers. It supports all subjects (e.g., Math, English, etc.) and due to several federal grants, has a huge repository of math content. ASSISTments is not just a math tutoring system. It is an "eco-system" of researchers, schools, parents, funders, and state partners, working together to help students. Duncan (2010) urged schools and teachers to use *formative assessment* information to inform their classroom instruction. The dilemma is that every minute spent testing is a minute taken away from instruction. ASSISTments alleviates this issue by tutoring students on items they get wrong, thus providing integrated assisting of students while they are being assessed. Teachers are using this detailed assessment data to adjust their classroom instruction and pacing. Several studies (e.g., Mendicino, Razzaq, & Heffernan, 2009; Singh, Saleem, Pradhan, Heffernan, Heffernan, Razzaq, & Dailey, 2011) demonstrate that ASSISTments lead to dramatically increased student knowledge when it is used for immediate feedback while student do their homework, compared to a control condition that represents traditional practice where students get feedback the next day in class. See http://www.assistments.org for free access to ASSISTments.

Electronic Portfolios. One of the most effective and widely used formative assessment tools is the electronic portfolio or e-folio. They have been used for many years to display collections of artifacts, including learning artifacts. Just as an artist may collect and show his portfolio of work, students and teachers are now using electronic programs like Adobe Acrobat Version X to electronically collect and share their academic work, thus often showing a progression of improvement and learning over time. An electronic portfolio can also include non-text-based artifacts of learning such as multimedia, web sites, drawings, audio recording, web site and electronic publications, thus presenting a full range of authentic assessment of the learning that has occurred.

One-to-One Computing. A U.S. Department of Education supported national study, Project RED (Revolting Education), surveyed principals and technology coordinators at 997 schools that implemented projects involving one personal computing device per student and those schools that did not have one-to-one computing but were also representative of U.S. education in terms of enrollment, geography, income, and ethnicity. With questions focused on 136 independent variables in 22 categories, the study analyzed a number of success factors including:

- High-stakes test scores;
- Disciplinary action and dropout rates;
- Teacher attendance;
- AP course enrollment and college attendance plans;
- Course completion and graduation rates for high school students; and
- Savings from such factors as reduced paperwork.

One-to-one computing schools were shown to significantly outperform schools that were not one-to-one computer supported (U.S. Department of Education Project RED Report, 2011).

The Project RED analysis also showed that having a principal who models and leads technology was the most important factor in high-performing one-to-one computing schools. A one-to-one computer-supported school greatly facilitated the use of technology for embedded assessment. However, a review of the literature by Abbitt (2011, p. 141) reports that "knowledge of technology is insufficient," by itself, to foster "successful technology integration" and that there is a complex interplay between knowledge of pedagogy and technology in understanding how teachers develop their ability to integrate technology into formative assessment and other classroom practices.

New Developments in Formative Assessment: Tools and Concepts. New tools and concepts are continually being developed that have implications for formative assessment. The following are some new developments to be watched for their impact on education.

Learning analytics. The push for individualized learning has helped drive more real-time analysis of how students are doing. According to Johnson, Smith, Willis, Levine, and Haywood, (2011) in the new Media Consortium, *The 2011 Horizon Report.* (2011, p. 26), the goal of learning analytics is to "enable teachers and schools to tailor educational opportunities to each student's level of need and ability." An example of how learning analytics works as a form of embedded assessment can be seen at Granville County Schools that have shown a 20% increase in graduation rates since implementing a learning analytics data analysis system. (http://www.converemag.com/policy/Granville-County-Schools-Creates-a-Technology-Culture.html).

Personal learning environments. This technology is often incorporated into learning management systems but can be separate as well. Personal learning environments allow students to direct their own learning by themselves or in groups. They generally involve a number of tools that learners choose to use as they learn. An example of a personal learning environment that uses an embedded assessment can be found at Creekview High School in Canton, Georgia, where sophomores learn how to configure Netvibes as a tool in their personal learning environment.

Flipped Classroom. Probably the best new example of how embedded assessments are being utilized is the Kahn Academy (http://www.khanacademy.org/about), which has developed a freely accessed library of 2,700 videos covering K–12 math, science topics such as biology, chemistry, and physics, and even reaches into the humanities with playlists on finance and history. Each video is a digestible chunk, approximately 10 minutes long and especially purposed for viewing on the computer. But more importantly, these videos come with an embedded assessment showing both individual and group progress in detail as students progress at their own pace from anywhere they have internet access. This project, funded in part by the Microsoft Foundation and the U.S. Department of Education, is currently free of charge and is often used at home in place of the teacher's in-class lecture, thus "flipping the classroom" and freeing up the teacher to provide and help on "homework" during school hours based on continuous individual assessment tracking.

Web 2.0 services and tools. Here are some other popular web tools that could also be used for embedded assessments.

1. Curriki brings teachers together to collaborate, share curriculum, and find new ideas or supplemental activities. This application facilitates the sharing of templates, study guides, handouts, and lesson plans.
2. Shmoop is an excellent tool that provides study guides for many disciplines including poetry, literature, civics, and U.S. history. The guides are geared toward children with enjoyable, understandable content.
3. ClassMarker makes quiz and test creation less time consuming. This online tool creates tests easily using short answer, true or false, multiple choice or essay questions, or a mix of question types. Teachers can randomize the questions and results can be provided instantaneously.
4. GradeFix helps students schedule time for homework around activities and commitments. The site is easy to use and helps students avoid the traps of procrastination and better allocate their time.
5. BrainHoney is a free resource allowing educators to personalize lesson plans, author curriculum, access grade books, and communicate with students and parents.
6. Engrade makes assessment efficient and classroom organization and reporting more achievable. Teachers can post assignment due dates, create student reports, and manage attendance and grade books.
7. ePals provides a database of classrooms around the world to connect to. It also provides controlled email translation tools and engaging learning projects to communicate safely with these globally connected classes and their individual students. This allows students to learn about other cultures and their educational practices and problems and collaborate on projects of global interest. Some students also use ePals to regularly practice and exchange language acquisition skills with native speakers. Language learning assessment does not get any more real than having to communicate with another student in their native language.
8. Wikis, web pages, and blogs work effectively to deliver learning and knowledge. They provide the student with the opportunity to contribute, reflect, and understand content.

By embedding assessment into one or more of these web 2.0 resources, not only can information be provided, but these internet tools can also serve as knowledge checks to reinforce learning. When used together, they are referred to as Mashups. For more information about Mashups and embedded assessment, see Eric Shepherd's blog at http://blog.eric.info/2012/05/a-model-and-assessment-the-7-minute-tutorial/

Summary

Real-time, embedded, formative assessment has been shown to be a powerful tool for teachers if implemented properly. Principals should promote this type of assessment. By utilizing real-time, embedded, formative assessment, good students continue to excel and struggling students gain success a step at a time, reducing their frustration and encouraging the desire to succeed. Traditional summative and state-sponsored tests remain important in the grand scope of evaluation, but teachers and administrators must learn the value of formative assessment and its impact on student achievement. In Michigan, a new law requires that 50% of teachers' and administrators' evaluations be based on student achievement. Implementing a continual program of formative assessment opens the achievement door for many students who have not been successful under traditional instructional and assessment procedures.

Endnote

1. Based on personal communication with Pat Davenport.

Annotated Bibliography

Marzano, R. (2010). *Formative assessment & standards-based grading: Classroom strategies that work.* Bloomington, IN: Marzano Research Laboratory. It provides an in-depth treatment of research-based instructional strategies that can be used in the classroom to enhance student achievement.

Moss, C. M., & Brookhart, S. (2009), *Advancing formative assessment in every classroom: A guide for instructional leaders. Association for Supervision and Curriculum Development,* Alexandria, VA. The authors provide ideas for principals for promoting formative assessment.

Popham, W. J. (2011). *Transformative assessment in action: An inside look at applying the process.* Alexandria, VA: Association for Supervision and Curriculum Development. Teachers can implement these formative assessment applications in the classroom.

Tools to assist principals in promoting real-time, embedded assessments. Kim Marshall has developed teacher evaluation rubrics covering all aspects of as teacher's job performance, including ways to implement formative assessments. Information on these rubrics can be found at www.marshallmemo.com and in the Kim Marshall article cited in the References of this chapter. Charlotte Danielson has developed an extensive teacher evaluation instrument that also focuses on formative assessment. More information on this rubric can be found at www.charlottedanielson.com and in the article cited in the References of this chapter.

References

Abbitt, J. T. (2011). An investigation of the relationship between self-efficacy beliefs about technology integration and technological pedagogical content knowledge (TPACK) among preservice teachers. *Journal of Digital Learning in Teacher Education, 27*(4), 134–143.

Anderson, R., & Dexter, S. (2005). School technology leadership: An empirical investigation of prevalence and effect. *Educational Administration Quarterly, 41*(1), 49–82.

Bakula, N. (2010). The benefits of formative assessments for teaching and learning. *Science Scope, 34*, 37–43.

Black, P., & Wiliam, D. (1998). Inside the black box: Raising standards through classroom assessment. *Phi Delta Kappan, 80*, 139–148.

Brookhart, S. (2008). *How to give effective feedback to your students.* Alexandria, VA: Association for Supervision and Curriculum Development.

Chappuis, S., & Chappuis, J. (2007). The best value in formative assessment. *Educational Leadership, 65*(4), 14–19.

Danielson, C. (1996). *Enhancing professional practice: A framework for teaching.* Alexandria, VA: Association for Supervision and Curriculum Development.

Dawson, C., & Rakes, G. C. (2003). The influence of principals' technology training on the integration of technology into schools. *Journal of Research on Technology in Education, 36*, 29–49.

Duncan, A. (2010). *Transforming American education: Learning powered by technology.* Washington, DC: U.S. Department of Education.

Feeney, E. J. (2007). Quality feedback: The essential ingredient for teacher success. *Clearing House: A Journal of Educational Strategies, Issues and Ideas, 80*(4), 191–197.

Garrison, C., & Ehringhaus, M. (2011). *Formative and summative assessments in the classroom.* Westerville, OH: National Middle School Association. Retrieved from November 28, 2011 http://www.amle.org/portals/0/pdf/publications/Web_Exclusive/Formative_Summative_Assessment.pdf

Hattie, J., & Timperley, H. (2007). The power of feedback. *Review of Educational Research, 77*, 81–112

Kellough, R. D., & Kellough, N. G. (1998). *Secondary school teaching: A guide to methods and resources, planning for competence.* Upper Saddle River, NJ: Prentice Hall.

Kimball, C., & Cone, T. (2002). Performance assessment in real time. *The School Administrator, 59*(4), 14–19.

Marshall, K. (2009). The why's and how's of teacher evaluation rubrics. *Edge, 2*(1), 1–19.

Marzano, R. (2003). *What works in schools: Translating research into action.* Alexandria, VA: Association for Supervision and Curriculum Development.

Marzano, R. (2010). *Formative assessment & standards-based grading: Classroom strategies that work.* Bloomington, IN: Marzano Research Laboratory.

Mendicino, M., Razzaq, L., & Heffernan, N. T. (2009). Comparison of traditional homework with computer supported homework. *Journal of Research on Technology in Education, 41*(3), 331–359.

Miranda, H. (2007). *Predictors of technology use in elementary classrooms: A multilevel SEM approach.* Paper presented at the 2007 American Educational Research Association Conference in Chicago, IL.

Miranda, H. P., & Russell, M. (2011). Understanding factors associated with teacher-directed student use of technology in elementary classrooms: A structural equation modeling approach. *British Journal of Educational Technology.* Published on-line on October 4, 2011. DOI: 10.1111/j.1467–8535.2011.01228.x.

O'Connor, C., & Mulchay, C. (2011). Feedback during web-based homework: The role of hints. In G. Biswas, S. Bull, J. Kay, & A. Mitrovic (Eds.), *Proceedings of the Artificial Intelligence in Education Conference 2011* (pp. 328–336). Springer. LNAI 6738.

Pausch, L. M., & Popp, M. P. (1997). *Assessment of information literacy: Lessons from the higher education assessment movement.* Retrieved July 16, 2012 from http://www.ala.org/acri/paperhtm/d30.html

Popham, W. J. (2008). Formative assessment: Seven stepping stones to success. *Principal Leadership, 9,* 16–20.

Russell, M., Bebell, D., O'Dwyer, L., & O'Connor, K. (2003). Examining teacher technology use: Implications for preservice and inservice teacher preparation. *Journal of Teacher Education, 54*(4), 297–310.

Schrock, K. (2011). *Informatic in education.* Presentation at the 4th International Society for Technology in Education, June 28, 2011, Philadelphia, PA.

Singh, R., Saleem, M., Pradhan, P., Heffernan, C., Heffernan, N., Razzaq, L., & Dailey, M. (2011). Improving K–12 homework with computers. AIED '11 Proceedings of the Artificial Intelligence in Education Conference. Springer. 328–336.

Stecker, P. M., Lembke, E. S., & Foegen, A. (2008). Using progress-monitoring data to improve instructional decision making. *Preventing School Failure, 52*(2), 48–58.

Stiggins, R. (2005). From formative assessment to assessment for learning: A path to success in standards-based schools. *Phi Delta Kappan, 87*(4), 324–328.

The New Media Consortium. (2011). *The New Horizon Report 2011–2012.* Retrieved July 13, 2012 from http://www.nmc.org/pdf/2011-Horizon-Report-K12.pdf

Ubben, G. C., Hughes, L. W., & Norris, C. J. (2011). *The principal: Creative leadership for excellence in schools.* Upper Saddle River, NJ: Pearson Education.

U.S. Department of Education, (2010), Project RED, The Technology Factor: Nine Keys to Student Achievement and Cost Effectiveness, found at http://www.pearsonfoundation.org/downloads/ProjectRED_TheTechnolgyFactor.pdf, retrieved April 2012.

8

Passion and Commitment for School Renewal

WALTER L. BURT

Introduction

The No Child Left Behind (NCLB) and Race to the Top (RTTT) legislations have pushed the issue of effective school leadership to the center of the school reform movement. Prior to the school accountability measures, the bulk of the conversation was exclusively focused on teachers. Although the majority of states have developed policies that call for improvements in curriculum standards, equity, teacher selection, development and recruitment, parent and community stakeholder involvement, as well as other pressing issues, most of these states have not developed equivalent measures for school leaders (Learning Point Associates, 2010). Year after year, school leaders face daunting challenges to improve student achievement. The prescription for making these changes, however, varies from district to district.

Each of the six previous dimensions has been laying the foundation for everything to come together as it should in this final chapter. The previous chapters have provided the learning-centered leadership tools principals must use to create a culture that supports high academic achievement for all students. These seven dimensions do not, in themselves, coalesce into elements that will produce the kind of dispositions and behaviors that will be internalized by all staff members. The research on school restructurings suggests that school renewal is no easy task

(Crum & Sherman, 2008; Halinger & Heck, 1996, 2010; Leithwood & Jantzi, 2000; Robinson et al., 2008; Smith et al., 2006; Witziers et al., 2003).

The preceding chapters focus more on the technical core of school renewal while this chapter on passion and commitment is most concerned with the moral core of school renewal. This final chapter hopes to bridge the gaps between each of the seven dimensions by examining the influence passion and commitment have on improving the academic achievement of all students.

This chapter's focus is on the evolution of leadership in educational institution from an historical and philosophical perspective, the moral imperative for school renewal, the impact passion and commitment has on creating a culture for improving student performance, and finally, the role principals must assume in forging change in an era of increased accountability.

Historical Perspective of Educational Leadership

There has been no other time in American history that the demand to improve student learning has become more evident. With this increasing demand, the focus on the principal to shepherd school improvement has become increasingly intensified. This crisis in education requires school administrators to become more adept in how they negotiate change. As schools become more diverse, in addition to increased insights about the knowledge and skills students will need, it becomes increasingly clear that school administrators will need to be able to lead in a more dynamic environment than any of their predecessors. As Cotton (2003) states, "Accountability for results is driving school reform in the United States, and it is central to improvement efforts in most other countries as well" (p. v). Principals work with and through other people to achieve organizational goals. An understanding of the behavior of people and the dispositions needed at work is fundamental to the success of the school's vision and goals.

This section will provide a brief historical overview of organizational principles that were developed in industrial organizations and how they have impacted the management and administration of public school institutions. Although these theories are discussed in a less than comprehensive fashion, they do offer a convenient way of discussing how these principles help to influence the thinking school administrators would need to lead schools in the future.

Classical Organizational Theory

Much of what we know about the management of schools and how people work within organizations was learned by studying the behavior of people in factories during the Industrial Revolution. As owners of companies had to deal with the challenging issues of being competitive, the scientific methods of inquiry provided answers about how to be both competitive and profitable (Carlson, 1996). The management system evolved by the manufacturing industries was based upon efficiency and effectiveness, and the bottom line for the organization was productivity. Non-monetary goals were secondary.

In an era of industrial expansion, engineers and scientists were responsible for developing machines and then combining them into assembly lines. Frederick Taylor, a top engineering consultant at the end of the 19th century, was responsible for solving production problems in factories all over the United States. With the development of Taylor's four "principles" of scientific management, he was able to formally differentiate the roles and responsibilities of workers and managers (Owens & Valesky, 2007; Glass, 2008). These principles led to the development of a system of supervision of workers in many different settings, including schools (Hoy & Miskel, 1987; Marion, 2002). According to Owens and Valesky (2007), the form of supervision that emerged in schools from this approach has not helped to support such concepts as collaboration and teamwork. They state:

> Taylor's principles still provide the justification for many school administrators and school board members to resist—openly or covertly—such ideas as collegial, collaborative approaches to goal setting, planning, and problem solving and other "bottom-up" approaches to school reform in favor of more traditional authoritarian approaches. (p. 87)

It is apparent that much of Taylor's work was concerned with matters related to analysis, synthesis, work ethics, efficiency, elimination of waste, and standardization of best practices. Early students of educational administration looked at Taylor's model of scientific management from the perspective of tasks that needed to be performed and monitored in the operation and administration of school responsibilities (Hoy & Miskel, 1987; Marion, 2002; Owens & Valesky, 2007).

Taylor's views on scientific management were clearly steeped in the need to hire "the right people," train them to work with the machine, align the expectations of the worker with the function of the machine, and provide financial incentives as motivation for increased productivity and performing work based upon the difficulty of the task (Owens & Valesky, 2007).

Bureaucracy Theory

Max Weber is associated with the development of the bureaucracy theory. As industrial organizations grew in the early 1900s, so did other forms of governmental and organizational institutions. In numerous instances, individuals were often associated with competing and complementing organizations. There were frequent conflicts such as labor unrests, revolution, and the rise of communism (Marion, 2002; Owens & Valesky, 2007).

Weber believed that the bureaucratic process should be less impersonal and irrational. He felt a bureaucracy would minimize the irrationality of large organizations in which the relationship between managers and workers was based on tradition and class, and the elimination of these practices would allow personnel within the organization to work in a less hostile environment.

The emphasis of the scientific management approach is most concerned with power and productivity while the bureaucratic approach to leadership is most concerned with organizational quality and the individual improvement of individuals. With the change in thinking about how to manage people within organization, a new theory of leadership would emerge that extols a different vision based on serving others instead of egoism and self-aggrandizement (Cerit, 2010, p. 303).

Human Relations Theory

The human relations movement developed as an outcry against the classical models of administration. Mary Parker Follet is considered responsible for emphasizing the human side of administration. Through her writings, she was able to share her beliefs about the problems within organizations. In this regard, she felt that the problem in all organizations was developing and maintaining dynamic and harmonious relationships (Bolman & Deal, 2008; Hoy & Miskel, 1987).

Human relations theory is attributed to the industrial psychologist Elton Mayo. He argues that scientific management does not consider the human element, and its failure to do so reduces productivity in the work environment. Mayo questioned deeply held assumptions of industrialists that workers had no rights beyond a paycheck and that their duty was to work hard and follow orders (Bolman & Deal, 2008). He is best known for his research associated with the Hawthorne Plant Studies, which concluded that, "Productivity was more a function of social conditions than of physical conditions—in stark contrast to the economic motivation assumed by scientific management" (Carlson, 1996, p.8) and for the first time questioned many of the assumptions made by engineers and administrative managers.

The research associated with the human relations theory led to additional research that dealt with the psychological needs of workers. A branch of research emerged that placed less emphasis on organizational structure and more emphasis on employee motivation and satisfaction as well as on group morale (Bolman & Deal, 2008; Carlson, 1996; Hoy & Miskel, 1987; Marion, 2002; Owens & Valesky, 2007).

The more notable researchers in this area were Carl Jung, associated with the human relations movement, Abraham Maslow (hierarchy of needs hypothesis), Douglas McGregor's conceptualization of motivation (Theory X and Theory Y), Frederick Herzberg's theory of hygienic motivators, and James MacGregor Burns' theory of transformational and transactional leaders.

Maslow, by far, is one of the most influential psychologists to develop a theory to explain human needs. His theory is based on the premise that, "People are motivated by a variety of wants, some more fundamental than others" (Bolman & Deal, 2008). Based upon these wants, Maslow grouped human needs based upon a hierarchy.

Building upon Maslow's hierarchy of needs theory, Douglas McGregor added an additional assumption that managers made about people tended to become self-fulfilling prophecies. In this regard, McGregor intimated that most supervisors either believed that subordinates are "lazy and passive," "have little ambition," "prefer to be led," and "resist change" (Theory X) or that, "The task of management is to arrange conditions so that people can achieve their own goals best by directing efforts toward organizational rewards" (Theory Y; (Bolman & Deal, 2008, p. 126).

It was James MacGregor Burns, the father of modern leadership theory, who is credited with establishing the terms and attributes associated with "transactional" and "transformational" leadership styles (Bass, 1985; Burns, 1978; Marzano et al., 2005). With respect to transactional leadership style, Burns (1978) describes a *"quid pro quo"* relationship between managers and workers.

Transformational leaders, on the other hand, are described by Burns (1978) in a more collaborative and descriptively engaging manner: In this matter, he states the following:

> Leadership occurs when one or more persons engage with others in such a way that leaders and followers raise one another to higher levels of motivation and morality. . . . Their purposes, which might have started out as separate but related, as in the case of transactional leadership, become fused. Power bases are linked not as counterweights but as mutual support for common purpose. Various

> names are used for such leadership, some of them derisory, elevating, mobilizing, inspiring, exalting, uplifting, preaching, exhorting, evangelizing. (p. 20)

Burns (1978) defines leadership as, "Leaders inducing followers to act for certain goals that represent the valucs and the motivations—the wants and needs, the aspirations and expectations—of both leaders and followers" (p. 19).

Systems Theory

A major breakthrough in understanding complexity in organizations is the concept of systems theory. Systems analysis is the application of this theory, and systems thinking is one of its tools. Systems theory is a departure from the hierarchical approach typically described in the industrial and bureaucratic models. A systems view recognizes that organizations, such as school systems, are deeply influenced by social interactions and interdependent relationships (Hoy & Miskel, 1987). The concept was first proposed by the biologist Ludwig von Bertalanffy in the 1940s. He suggested that there is degree of isomorphism between biological systems and human organizations. In this regards, he argued that "real" systems are open to and interact with their respective environments (Bertalanffy, 1968).

It was the work of W. Edwards Deming, the father of Total Quality Management (TQM), that literally transformed the work environment in manufacturing companies as well as educational institutions (Aguayo, 1990; Deming, 1994; Marzano, Waters, & McNulty, 2005; Marsh, Pane, & Hamilton, 2006; Senge, 1990). His famous theory of profound knowledge, including 14 points for creating a more efficient workplace, helped to shift top-down decision-making to a more collaborative relationship between managers and employees through five basic steps: change agency, teamwork, continuous improvement, trust building, and eradication of short-term goals (Deming, 1994; Walman, 1993, as cited in Marzano, et al., 2005, p. 15).

In public school settings where continuous change is becoming the norm, the organization faces new challenges of constant learning to its ability to learn. Fritz (1999) suggests that organizations follow inescapable structural laws, and they have no choice to do other because they must follow a path of least resistance. He suggests that, "The principle of structural tension—knowing what we want to create and knowing where we are in relationship to our goals—is the most powerful force an organization can have" (p. 30). One can convincingly argue that it is the role of successful organizational leaders to create structural tension within the organization, particularly as it relates to identified gaps between the goals of the organization and current reality.

Changing an organization is a very complex process and requires a tremendous amount of "heavy lifting" on the part of leaders who are engaged in this endeavor (Panasonic Foundation, 1999). Schools have often been expected to improve with staff development training. A frequent and compelling argument has been that improving student performance depends largely upon the ability of the organization itself to improve.

Systems thinking is gaining a great deal of popularity in this era of school reform. A greater understanding of the dynamic interactions in educational organizations is crucial if educators are to make decisions about school reform efforts that are likely to succeed. Many organizational leaders, including leaders from school districts, are finding that the discipline of systems thinking "provides a framework for clarifying and deepening their understanding of dynamic systems and for organizing their thoughts and strategies in leading and managing school system change" (Panasonic Foundation, 1999, p. 1).

With current advancements in the field of cybernetics, and its particular emphasis on the study of information, communication, and control, a series of questions have emerged as to whether modern organizations are capable of learning in an ongoing way (Morgan, 2006). Many complex systems are able to detect and correct errors and, consequently, influence the rules that govern their operating norms. This type of action is symbolic of organizations that are able to self-question and is a prerequisite of the ability of organizations to learn and self-organize.

It was Peter Senge (1990; Senge et al., 2000) and his seminal work, *The Fifth Discipline,* in which the concept of a learning organization and systems thinking as applied to organizations, first emerged. Senge (1990) offers the following description of systems thinking: "It is a discipline for seeing wholes. It is a framework for seeing interrelationships rather than things, for seeing patterns of change rather than static 'snapshots' " (p. 68). He argues that if organizations are to be successful in a competing and global market, they need to make use of a learning approach, a process that is not usually taken in a traditional authoritarian organization.

How are these organizational/leadership theories related to the issue of passion and commitment for school renewal? The following section sheds light on this important question.

The Moral Imperative for School Renewal

Teachers, principals, and parents know from personal experience that principals make a difference in the lives of children. Today, educational leaders face a tremendous challenge that drastically impedes the progress of students. Staff and students are impacted by issues related to the increase in technology, dwindling economy, a demand from schools to be more accountable for student achievement, the need for greater choice in school enrollment, issues of equity, and the need for greater collaboration between the business community, schools, and agencies serving children that have social, economical, and learning disabilities. These issues place a considerable amount of pressure on practicing school administrators to the extent that many school leaders are reluctant to act (Cooley & Shen, 1999; Fullan, 2003; Shen, Cooley, & Wegenke, 2004). Fullan (2004) maintains: "Today's leaders face a dilemma: failing to act when the environment is radically changing leads to extinction, yet making quick decisions under conditions of seeming chaos can be equally fatal" (p. xiii).

The primary purpose of leadership in education is to make a difference in the lives of children. Collectively speaking, the moral purpose of education is to ensure that all children learn, that steps are taken to reduce the achievement gap between students based upon race, ethnicity, gender, socio economic conditions, and that what children learn will enable them to be productive workers and citizens in society (Fullan, 2003). If staff, students, and parents are not treated in a fair and equitable manner, then you will be a leader without followers (Fullan, 2001). In essence, organizational life is better served in the long run by moral leadership (Burns, 1978; Kouzes & Posner, 2002).

So what is the role of leadership in those who are responsible for managing change? According to Fullan (2004), "Leadership is not mobilizing others to solve problems we already know how to solve, but helping them to confront problems that have not yet been addressed successfully" (pp. 2–3). His model for leadership can best be described in the following list:

1. Moral purpose
2. Understanding change
3. Building relationships
4. Creating and sharing knowledge
5. Making coherence

According to Kouzes and Posner (2002), "Leadership practices per se are amoral. But leaders—the men and women who use the practices—are moral or immoral" (p. 393). What is obvious to school leaders is that in a culture of change there are no correct answers and solutions. Some critics assert that, "The burden for school improvement in a time of accountability falls squarely on the shoulders of principals" (Crum & Sherman, 2008). Yet, the key to creating and sustaining successful educational organizations for the 21st century is leadership. Kotter (1996) makes the following observation: "The twenty-first century employee will need to know more about leadership and management than did his or her twentieth-century counterpart. . . . Without these skills, dynamic, adaptive enterprises are not possible" (p. 176).

It was the effective school research of the late 1970s that produced findings about the nature and importance of principals' influence on student achievement (Cotton, 2003; Edmonds, 1979). Subsequently, there has been a plethora of research on school leadership and the influence principals have on student achievement (Cotton, 2003; Edmonds, 1979; Halinger & Heck, 1996, 2010; Leithwood & Jantzi, 1999; Marks & Printy, 2003; Marzano et al., 2005; Robinson, Lloyd, & Rowe, 2008; Sergiovanni, 1995).What is apparent from the existing body of research is that leadership practices vary from school to school, and distilling these key practices down to a theory of action has been very difficult to do so. Trying to unravel this effect of principals and instructional leadership practices is a very complicated process (Crum & Sherman, 2008; Halinger & Heck, 1996, 2010).

The research pertaining to the influence principals have on student performance is not conclusive. Although Cotton (2003) suggests that extraordinary principals embody all, or nearly all, of the traits and actions of principals in successful schools, Robinson et al.(2008) cautions that "such an interpretation would reinforce the highly problematic heroic approach to school leadership" (p. 669). Schools tend to be at different stages of development, and each will require a different leadership emphasis (Robinson et al., 2008).

Passion and Commitment for School Renewal

There is a growing body of research findings that suggest exemplary leaders have a greater passion and commitment for their staffs, students, parents, their building, and district. Caring for others and their well-being conveys a sense of conviction and responsibility to others. Exemplary leaders model the expectations they have for others and are willing to make personal sacrifices to demonstrate their willingness and conviction to make improvements within their organization (Burt &

McCrumb, 2011; Kouzes & Posner, 2002). Exemplary leaders have a passion for their organizations that transcend both fame and fortune (Kouzes & Posner, 2002). According to Kouzes and Posner (2002):

> Caring is at the heart of leadership. . . . We also know that true leaders care about something much bigger than themselves and much bigger than all of us. Leaders care about making a difference in the world. If you don't care deeply for and about something and someone, then how can you expect others to feel any sense of conviction? How can you expect others to get jazzed, if you're not energized and excited? How can you expect others to suffer through the long hours, hard work, absences from home, and personal sacrifices if you're not similarly committed? (p. 116)

The current research on principal leadership suggests that there are a number of dimensions associated with principal leadership (Crum & Sherman, 2008; Halinger & Heck, 1996, 2010; Marks & Printy, 2003; Robinson et al., 2008; Smith et al., 1996; Sebring & Bryk, 2000). Principals in high performing schools display certain attributes that separate them from their corresponding counterparts that do not incorporate, or implement to a lesser degree, certain leadership dimensions.

Cerit (2010) posits that organizational commitment involves making an effort to embrace the organization's aim and values as a member of the organization. Committed employees feel the need to go beyond normal job expectations. They tend to have the following traits and characteristics:

1. A strong belief in and acceptance of the organization's goals and values;
2. A willingness to exert considerable effort on behalf of the organization, and;
3. A definite desire to maintain organizational membership (Mowday et al., 1982, as cited by Cerit, 2010, p. 304).

The research of Kouzes and Posner (2002) supports this contention. They identified five practices and 10 corresponding leadership behaviors, or commitment attributes, which can serve as the basis for learning to lead.

School and district effectiveness studies show that high levels of student achievement are possible when schools and the district act as coordinated units of change. Chrispeels, Burke, Johnson, and Daly (2008) found that with professional development, school leadership teams could serve as an important bridge between the central office and the schools in ways that can enhance coordination, depth, spread, and commitment to district reforms.

Hulpia, Devos, and Rosseel (2009) investigated the relationship between distributed leadership, the cohesion of the leadership team, participative decision-making, context variables, and the organizational commitment and job satisfaction of teachers and teacher leaders. Multiple regression and path analyses revealed that the study variables explained the significant amount of variance in organizational commitment. The amount of explained variance for job satisfaction was considerably lower when compared to organizational commitment. Most striking was that the cohesion of the leadership team and the amount of leadership support was strongly related to organizational commitment and indirectly to job satisfaction. Decentralization of leadership functions was weakly related to organizational commitment and job satisfaction. Bogler (2005) examined the mediating effect of teacher empowerment on the relationship between teachers' participation in decision making and their professional commitment. Hierarchical regression analyses revealed that teacher empowerment mediated the effect of teachers' participation in decision making on teacher commitment. Findings in these studies help to explain the importance of passion and commitment when implementing school reform initiatives.

Moller, Vedoy, Presthus, and Skedsmo (2009) conducted a study to determine whether and how success had been sustained over time in schools that were identified as successful. Findings in this study revealed that the learning-centered approach that had been sustained in the successful school resulted in higher student achievement than those schools where there had been changes in leadership. Lance (2010) studied two ethnically diverse urban primary schools in England. Both schools had been recognized locally and nationally. Findings in this study suggested that the commitment of teachers to their individual schools, their respect for students and their families, and their attention to providing a breadth of learning experience were key factors to their success. Day (2004) conducted research on 10 successful and experienced teacher leaders in both urban and suburban school districts. The research revealed that the 10 teacher leaders sustained their success of essential leadership qualities, skills, and principles, and these practices enabled them to handle a number of tensions and dilemmas associated with the management of change. Fundamental to their success was their passion for students, school, and community. Ma, Shen, Kavanaugh, Lu, Brandi, Goodman, Till, and Watson (2011) studied the efficacy of a staff development program in multiple early childhood centers. Findings in this study suggested that educational leaders need to be patient when implementing an initiative because it may take time to see the results of the intervention. Thus, passion and commitment are important for staying the course and seeing results.

Rogers (1995) found that adopters or innovators can be categorized as either innovators (2.5%), early adopters (13.5%), members of the early majority (34%), members of the late majority (34%), and laggards (16%)—all based upon the mathematically based normal distribution. He suggests that each adopter's willingness and ability to adopt any initiative depend on their awareness, interest, evaluation, trial, and adoption. Findings in this study suggest the need for organizational leaders to identify and consider those individuals who display both passion and commitment for school reform initiatives. Rogers suggests that early adopters are more likely to be committed to organization improvement.

Lee, Levin, and Soler (2005) in their study of the implementation of accelerated schools in Hong Kong, China, found that change is slow and that the commitment of the principal and a core group is critical to change. Cerit (2010) examined the effects of servant leadership behaviors of primary school principals on teachers' school commitment. Findings in this study revealed that there was a significant and positive relationship between servant leadership behaviors of principals and the teachers' commitment to school. Servant leadership was a significant predictor of teachers' school commitment. Dewettinck and Ameijde (2011) investigated the relationship between leadership empowerment behavior (LEB), employee psychological empowerment, and employee attitudes (affective commitment and job satisfaction) and behavioral intentions (staff willingness to stay with the job). This study found a direct relationship between leadership empowerment behavior and job satisfaction and affective commitment. Psychological empowerment partially mediates these relationships. Employee attitudes were also shown to be related to employees' intention to stay with the organization.

Although the dimension of passion and commitment is vital to school renewal, Blackmore's study (2004) in Australia provides insight into challenges school leaders may face as they implement school renewal initiatives. Blackmore found that accountability initiatives were often seen by teachers and principals to be distractions; more about reporting and recording, rather than addressing substantive educational issues. These measures distanced teachers and leaders from the "real" and "passionate" work of education while distancing teachers and principals' emotions and desires to do well. In that sense, performativity ("being seen to be good") and passion ("for doing good") often produced counterintuitive impulses.

Other examples of passion and commitment may be reflected in these dimensions of leadership: self-efficacy, taking risk, safe and orderly school environment, visioning and goal setting, visibility, positive and supportive climate, shared leadership, decision making, staff empowerment, risk-taking, and collaboration. Several of these dimensions are described below. Although the behaviors are reported separately, many of them do not exist in isolation but may be found in combination with others.

Self-Efficacy

In high-achieving schools, principals hold themselves accountable for student achievement. They believe in themselves and feel they can persist through difficulties, setbacks, and failures (Cotton, 2003). In a study conducted by Smith, Guarino, Strom, and Adams (2006), they found that principals' self-efficacy beliefs tended to increase with the complexity of the job and that they were more productive when they were able to facilitate an effective teaching and learning environment.

Safe and Orderly School Environment

The earliest study on school effectiveness found that the principal's role in establishing a safe and orderly environment was key to a high-performing school (Edmonds, 1979). Leadership that ensures a safe and orderly environment makes it possible for teaching and learning. Findings by Robinson et al. (2008) suggest that, "Leaders' involvement in teacher learning provides them with a deep understanding of the conditions required to make and sustain the changes required for improved outcomes" (p. 668).

Vision and Goals Focused on High Levels of Student Learning

There is an abundance of research that supports the notion that a principal's strong focus on academics is essential to improving student achievement (Cotton, 2003; Leithwood & Jantzi, 1999). Defining and communicating the mission of the school are also important (Witzierset al., 2003). Robinson et al. (2008) found that goal setting is a powerful tool for improving valued student outcomes because it signals to staff that even though everything is important, some activities and outcomes are more important. Without clear goals, staff effort and initiatives can be dissipated in multiple agendas and conflicting priorities (Kouzes & Posner, 2002; Robinson et al., 2008).

Visibility and Accessibility

In high-achieving schools the principals spend their time in classrooms, hallways, lunchroom, and meeting with instructional leadership teams rather than cloistered in their offices. In a study by Witziers et al. (2003) on specific leadership behaviors of administrators, the findings show that effect sizes, small but significant, tended to occur in several leadership behaviors: supervision and evaluation ($Z_r = .02$), monitoring ($Z_r = .07$), visibility ($Z_r = .07$), and defining and communicating mission ($Z_r = .19$).

Positive and Supportive School Climate

Arguably, the leadership provided by a principal contributes to the school climate. Principal leadership makes a difference in influencing internal school practices associated with student learning. These practices are associated with developing personnel and facilitating leadership. Principals in these schools empower staff members and delegate responsibility in many different ways. They hold themselves and their staff accountable for student success and they communicate and facilitate instruction and managing change (Cotton, 2003; Crum & Sherman, 2008; Halinger & Heck, 1996). Chi, Chung, and Tsai's (2011) research pertaining to the relationship between leader-positive moods and team performance found that leader-positive moods not only directly enhanced team performance but also indirectly led to improved team performance through the explicit mediating process (i.e., transformational leadership) and the implicit mediating process (i.e., positive group affective tone).

Shared Leadership, Decision Making, and Staff Empowerment

There is a growing body of research that suggests when principals empower their staffs through shared leadership and decision-making authority, it supports learning within the organization (Cotton, 2003; Senge, 1999, 2000) and improves student achievement. Marks and Printy (2003) found that strong transformational leadership by the principal is essential in supporting the commitment of teachers and getting them involved in the implementation of various instructional and support initiatives in the school.

Halinger and Heck (2010) examined the effects of collaborative leadership on school improvement and student reading achievement in 192 elementary schools over a four-year time period. Findings in this study showed a significant and direct effect of collaborative leadership on change in the schools' academic capacity and indirect effects on rates of growth in student reading achievement.

Keung (2008) examined the causal relationship between teacher participation in decision making and their affective outcome for developing a participatory decision making model and identified the decision domains that would assist school administrators to effectively involve teachers in decision making under the school-based management policy. The results showed that a multi-dimensional model was identified, that the relationships among the variables of the model were also explored. The three-dimensional decision model includes instructional, curriculum, and managerial domains; and the variables of the affective outcome include job satisfaction, job commitment, and perception of workload. All the affective outcomes were related to the form and extent of teachers' participation in decision making.

Risk-Taking

Sebring and Bryk (2000) and Marks and Printy (2003) found that principals in effective schools skillfully use a number of strategies to get new and innovative instructional strategies implemented. Williams, Tabernik, and Krivak's (2009) study of superintendents found that their commitment and support empowered teachers to risk change and provided them with effective teaching tools and methods.

Collaboration

Robinson et al. (2008) found that leaders in schools where students performed above expected levels were more likely to be involved with their staff in curriculum planning, visiting classrooms, and reviewing evidence about student learning. Hallinger and Heck (2010) found that collaborative leadership positively impacted student learning indirectly by building the academic capacity of staffs. Although networking is becoming an increasingly popular school improvement strategy, there has been little research to show the challenges school leaders face as they enter into these new relationships. In a study conducted by Evans and Stone-Johnson (2010) they found that head teachers faced three types of challenges: contextual considerations for network involvement, building internal commitment and capacity for network participation, and balancing network activities with other school reform efforts. The research suggests that networking can be learned and that the presence of a support system for network leaders may enhance the effectiveness and quality of participation for both individual schools and the network at large.

The Role of Principals in a School Renewal Environment

The success of school renewal initiatives will be dependent upon how quickly schools will be able to determine how well these initiatives are working and whether there is a need for staff to redirect its efforts when new initiatives are not progressing as planned. In this regard, Fullan (2003) challenges all who work in education to rethink the critical role of the principal as a school leader in the current era of accountability.

The significance of leadership in implementing change is a widely accepted axiom. The complexity of managing schools today makes the traditional "single person" leadership model obsolete and somewhat anachronistic (Bolman & Deal, 2008; Carlson, 1996; Cotton, 2003; Edmonds, 1979; Deming, 1994; Fritz, 1999; Hallinger & Heck, 1996, 2010; Kouzes & Posner, 2002; Leithwood & Jantzi, 1999; Marks & Printy, 2003, Marzano et al., 2005; Robinson et al., 2008; Senge, 1990, 2000).

To be effective, principals must ensure that effective steps are put in place to ensure that the mission of the organization is aligned with organizational goals (Fritz, 1999; Fullan, 2004; Morgan, 2006; Senge, 1999, 2000). According to Angus (1989), these practices may include establishing an atmosphere of order, discipline, purpose, creating a climate of high expectations for staff and students, encouraging collegial and collaborative relationships, and building commitment among staff and students to the school's goals, facilitating teachers in spending maximum time on direct instruction, encouraging staff development and valuation, and being a dynamic instructional leader (Duignan, 1986, as cited by Angus, 1989, p. 66).

Today, school turnaround models are becoming very popular as possible solutions to improving America's worst-performing schools (Hess & Gift, 2009; Murphy, 2008). Although these models bring hope to improving low-performing schools in a relatively short period of time, there is the need for school leaders who will make this work possible. According to Murphy (2008), it is necessary to recognize that the leadership within organizations must be strengthened. It is about leaders who are willing to create a culture of change, usually in complex situations. According to Fullan (2004):

> It is not about being a superleader. Charismatic leaders inadvertently often do more harm than good because, at best, they provide episodic improvement followed by frustrated or despondent dependence. Superleaders usually are role models who cannot be emulated by most other people but deep and sustained reform depends on many of us, not just on the extraordinary few. (pp. 1–2)

Resources to Assess and Improve Passion and Commitment

Listed below are several resources that may be used by individuals who are interested in assessing one's own and others' passion and commitment for school reform.

Leading Questions

Leadership is all about creating a vision and motivating others towards the vision. However, the instrument of leadership is the self, and mastery of the art of leadership comes from the mastery of self (Kouzes & Posner, 2002, pp. 390–391). As one takes on additional responsibilities to lead individuals within an organization, there are a number of questions to ask oneself. For example:

- How certain am I of my own conviction about the vision and values?
- What gives me the courage to continue in the face of uncertainty and adversity?
- How will I handle disappointments, mistakes, and setbacks?
- What are my strengths and weaknesses?
- What do I need to do to improve my abilities to move the organization forward?
- How solid is my relationship with my constituents?
- How can I keep myself motivated and encouraged?
- What keeps me from giving up?
- Am I the right one to be leading at this very moment? Why?
- How much do I understand about what is going on in the organization and the world in which it operates?
- How prepared am I to handle the complex problems that now confront my organization?
- What are my beliefs about how people ought to conduct the affairs of our organization?
- Where do I think the organization ought to be headed over the next ten years? (Kouzes & Posner, 2002, p. 392)

Self-Assessment of Servant Leadership Profile Instrument

This instrument was designed for individuals to monitor themselves on several leadership characteristics by indicating their level of agreement (strongly disagree to strongly agree) on various aspects of leadership. The instrument contains 12 different subscales: Integrity, Humility, Servanthood, Caring for Others, Empowering Others, Developing Others, Visioning, Goal Setting, Leading, Modeling, Team Building, and Shared Decision-Making. The reader can go to http://hci2010mmp.wiki.hci.edu.sg/fi . . . +Framework.pdf to view a copy of this instrument.

Annotated Bibliography for Suggested Reading

The increased demand for school accountability has produced a lot of "band-aid" solutions about how this work should be done. Senge (1999, 2000) warns educational leaders about "quick fixes" and adopting a "program of the week" mentality. What are so sorely needed in our schools are individuals who are most concerned about "doing the job," rather than "maintaining" the job. To this end, I have provided the following list of resources that current and practicing administrators can rely upon to improve teaching and learning in their respective schools.

Learning Point Associates. (2010). *What experiences from the field tell us about school leadership and turnaround: A district and school improvement thought paper.* Washington, DC. This paper describes how school leaders can turn around persistently low-performing schools.

Bolman, L. G., & Deal, T. E. (2008). *Reframing organizations: Artistry, choice, and leadership.* San Francisco: Jossey-Bass. This book provides the reader with a process for looking at organizations through four different lenses. They are: structural, human resource, political, and symbolic frames.

Burns, J. M. (1978). *Leadership.* New York: Harper & Row Publishers, Inc. This book discusses the power and structure of leadership and the many different attributes of people in leadership positions.

Fullan, M., & Ballew, A. C. (2004). *Leading in a culture of change: Personal action guide and workbook.* San Francisco: Jossey-Bass. This book presents a flexible and effective strategy for managers to make decisions in a constantly changing environment.

Kouzes, J. M., & Posner, B. Z. (2002). *The leadership challenge.* San Francisco: Jossey-Bass. This book provides a thorough portrayal of leadership and practical suggestions for addressing difficult situations.

Senge, P., Cambron-McCabe, M., Lucas, T., Smith, B., Dutton, J., & Kleiner, A. (2000). *Schools that learn: A fifth discipline fieldbook for educators, parents, and everyone who cares about education.* New York: Doubleday Publishing Company. This book presents learning organization principles through articles and case studies designed to kindle the fire of school improvement.

Conclusion

Principal leadership is both an exciting and intimidating field of work. Although there are literally thousands of books written on this subject, the attributes of leadership can be distilled into three distinct categories: creating a vision for the organization, motivating people to incorporate the vision, and developing people to work towards the vision.

Much of what we know about school leadership came from industry where the emphasis was about managing people and resources, organizational effectiveness, and productivity. School administrators are still concerned with many of these managerial responsibilities, but the role of leadership has shifted dramatically over the years from managing people to creating an environment where shared responsibility and collaboration are fostered.

There are numerous dimensions of leadership. If change is going to occur within schools, school leaders must have the passion and commitment to do this important work. The concern must be about "doing the work" rather than "maintaining the job." The current research on the impact of principal leadership, and its influence on student achievement, provides ample evidence to support the claim that leadership has a significant indirect influence on school practices that are associated with increased student learning.

References

Aguayo, R. (1990). *Dr. Deming: The American who taught the Japanese about quality.* New York: Fireside.

Angus, L. (1989). 'New' leadership and the possibility of educational reform. In John Smyth (Ed.) *Critical perspectives on education leadership* (pp. 43–168). New York: Falmer.

Bass, B. M. (1990). From transactional to transformational leadership. *Organizational Dynamics, 16*(3), 19–31.

Bertalanffy, L. V. (1968). *General system theory: Foundations, development, applications.* New York: George Braziller, Inc.

Blackmore, J. (2004). Restructing educational leadership in changing contexts: A local/global account of restructuring in Australia. *Journal of Educational Change, 5*(3), 267–288

Bogler, R. (2005). The power of empowerment: Mediating the relationship between teachers' participation in decision-making and their professional commitment. *Journal of School Leadership, 15*(1), 76–98.

Bolman, L. G., & Deal, T. E. (2008). *Reframing organizations: Artistry, choice, and leadership.* San Francisco: Jossey-Bass.

Burns, J. M. (1978). *Leadership.* New York: Harper & Row.

Burt, W., & McCrumb, D. (2011). Tenure of African American superintendents: A forty-year recapitulation of the Michigan experience. *JABSE, 9*(1), 36–53.

Carlson, R. V. (1996). *Reframing & reform: Perspectives on organization, leadership, and school change.* White Plains, NY: Longman Publishers, Inc.

Cerit, Y. (2010). The effects of servant leadership on teachers' organizational commitment in primary schools in Turkey. *International Journal of Leadership in Education, 13*(3), 301–317.

Chi, N., Chung, Y., & Tsai, W. (2011). How do happy leaders enhance team success? The mediating roles of transformational leadership, group affective tone, and team processes. *Journal of Applied Social Psychology, 41*(6), 1421–1454.

Chrispeels, J., Burke, P., Johnson, P., & Daly, A. (2008). Aligning mental models of district and school leadership teams for reform coherence. *Education and Urban Society,* 40(6), 730–750.

Cooley, V. E., & Shen, J. (1999). Who will lead?: The top 10 factors that influence teachers moving into administration. *NASSP Bulletin, 83*(606), 75–80.

Cotton, K. (2003). *Principals and student achievement: What the research says.* Alexandria, VA: Association for Supervision and Curriculum Development.

Crum, K. S., & Sherman, W. H. (2008). Using effective schools research to promote culturally competent leadership practices. *Journal for Effective Schools, 16*(4), 367–389.

Day, C. (2004). The passion of successful leadership. *School Leadership & Management, 24*(4), 425–437.

Deming, W. E. (1994). *The new economics.* Cambridge, MA: MIT's Center for Advanced Educational Services.

Dewettinck, K., & Ameijde, M. (2011). Linking leadership empowerment behavior to employee attitudes and behavioural intentions: Testing the mediating role of psychological empowerment. *Personnel Review, 40*(3), 284–305.

Edmonds, R. (1979). Some schools work and more can. *Social Policy, 9*(2), 28–32.

Evans, M., & Stone-Johnson, C. (2010). Internal leadership challenges of network participation. *International Journal of Leadership in Education. 13*(2), 203–220.

Fritz, R. (1999). *The path of least resistance for managers: Designing organizations to succeed.* San Francisco: Berrett-Koehler.

Fullan, M. (2001). *Leading in a culture of change.* San Francisco: Jossey-Bass.

Fullan, M. (2003). *The moral imperative of school leadership.* Thousand Oaks, CA: Corwin.

Fullan, M. (2004). *Leading in a culture of change: Personal action guide and workbook.* San Francisco: Jossey-Bass.

Glass, G. V. (2008). *Fertilizers, pills, and magnetic strips: The fate of public education in America.* Charlotte, NC: Information Age.

Halinger, P., & Heck, R. H. (1996). Reassessing the role of the principal's role in school effectiveness: A review of empirical research, 1980–1995. *Educational Administration Quarterly, 32*(1), 5–44.

Halinger, P., & Heck, R. H. (2010). Leadership for learning: Does collaborative leadership make a difference in school improvement? *Educational Management Administration & Leadership, 38*(6), 654–678.

Hess, F. M., & Gift, T. (2009). *School turnarounds: Resisting the hype, giving them hope.* Washington, DC: American Enterprise Institute for Public Policy Research.

Hoy, W. H., & Miskel, C. G. (1987). *Educational administration: Theory, research, and practice* (3rd ed.). New York: Random House.

Hulpia, H., Devos, G., & Rosseel, Y. (2009). The relationship between the perception of distributed leadership in secondary schools and teachers' and teacher leaders' job satisfaction and organizational commitment. *School Effectiveness and School Improvement, 20*(3), 291–317.

Keung, C. (2008). The effect of shared decision-making on the improvement in teachers' job development. *New Horizons in Education, 56*(3), 31–46.

Kotter, J. P. (1996). *Leading change: An action plan from the world's foremost expert on business leadership.* Boston: Harvard Business School Press.

Kouzes, J. M., & Posner, B. Z. (2002). *The leadership challenge.* San Francisco: Jossey-Bass.

Lance, A. (2010). A case study of two schools: Identifying core values conducive to the building of a positive school culture. *Management in Education, 24*(3), 118–123.

Learning Point Associates (2010 December). *What experiences from the field tell us about school leadership and turnaround: A district and school improvement thought paper.* Naperville, Il: Learning Point Associates. Retrieved June 6, 2011, from http://www.learningpt.org/pdfs/leadership_turnaround_schools.pdf

Lee, J. C., Levin, H., & Soler, P. (2005). Accelerated schools for quality education: A Hong Kong perspective. *The Urban Review, 37*(1), 63–81.

Leithwood, K., & Jantzi, D. (1999). The relative effects of principal and teacher sources of leadership on student engagement with school. *Educational Administration Quarterly, 35,* 679–706.

Ma, X., Shen, J., Kavanaugh, A., Lu, X., Brandi, K., Goodman, J., Till, L., & Watson, G. (2011). Effects of quality improvement system on child care centers. *Journal of Research in Childhood Education, 25* (4), 399–414.

Marion, R. (2002). *Leadership in education: Organizational theory for practitioners.* Long Grove, IL: Waveland.

Marks, H. M., & Printy, S. (2003). Principal leadership and school performance: Integration of transformational and instructional leadership. *Educational Administration Quarterly,* 39, 370–397.

Marsh, J. A., Pane, J. F., & Hamilton, S. (2006). *Making sense of data-driven decision making in education: Evidence from recent Rand research.* Rand Corporation.

Marzano, R. J., Waters, T., & McNulty, B. A. (2005). *School leadership that works: From research to results.* Aurora, CO: McREI.

Moller, J, Vedoy, G., Presthus, A. M., & Skedsmo, G. (2009). Successful principalship in Norway: Sustainable ethos and incremental change? *Journal of Educational Administration, 47*(6), 731–741.

Morgan, G. (2006). *Images of organizations.* Thousand Oaks, CA: Sage.

Murphy, J. (2008). The place of leadership in turnaround schools: Insights from organizational recovery in the public and private sectors. *Journal of Educational Administration, 46*(1), 74–98.

Owens, R. G., & Valesky, T. C. (2007). *Organizational behavior in education: Adaptive leadership and school reform.* Boston, MA: Pearson Education, Inc.

Panasonic Foundation. (1999). *Systems thinking: Untangling the Gordian knots of systemic change. Strategies.* Secaucus, NJ: Panasonic Foundation.

Robinson, V. M. J., Lloyd, C. A., & Rowe, K. J. (2008). The impact of leadership on student outcomes: An analysis of the differential effects of leadership types. *Educational Administration Quarterly, 44*(5), 635–674.

Rogers, E. M. (1995). *Diffusion of innovations* (4th ed.). New York: The Free Press.

Sebring, P. B., & Bryk, A. S. (2000). School leadership and the bottom line in Chicago. *Phi Delta Kappan, 81*(6), 440–444.

Senge, P. (1990). *The fifth discipline: The art & practice of the learning organization.* New York: Doubleday.

Senge, P., Cambron-McCabe, N., Lucas, T., Smith, B., Dutton, J., & Kleiner, A. (2000). *Schools that learn: A fifth discipline fieldbook for educators, parents, and everyone who cares about education.* New York: Doubleday.

Sergiovanni, T. J. (1995). *The principalship: A reflective practice perspective* (3rd ed.). Needham Heights, MA: Allyn and Bacon.

Shen, J., Cooley, V., & Wegenke, G. (2004). Perspectives on factors influencing application of principalship. A comparative study of teachers, principals, and superintendents. *Internationl Journal of Leadership in Education, 7*(1), 57–70.

Smith, W., Guarino, A., Strom, P., & Adams, O. (2006). Effective teaching and learning environments and principal self-efficacy. *Journal of Research for Educational Leaders, 3*(2), 4–23.

Williams, P., Tabernik, A., & Krivak, T. (2009). The power of leadership, collaboration, and professional development. *Education and Urban Society, 41*(4), 437–456.

Witziers, B., Bosker, R. J., & Kruger, M. L. (2003). Educational leadership and student achievement: The elusive search for an association. *Educational Administration Quarterly, 39*(3) 398–425.

Index

–C–

-D-

-E-

-F-

-G-

-H-

-I-

-J-

-K-

–L–

–M–

–N–

–O–

–P–

-Q-

-R-

-S-

–T–

–U–

–V–

–W–

-Y-

-Z-